NOR IRON BARS A CAGE

MA THANEGI

Nor Iron Bars a Cage
By Ma Thanegi

Copyright ©2013 ThingsAsian Press

Edited by Janet Brown
Copy-editing by Sheri Quirt

Cover: Red Gate, by Ma Thanegi

ThingsAsian Press
3230 Scott Street San Francisco, California 94123 USA
www.thingsasianpress.com

Printed in Hong Kong

ISBN-10: 1-934159-50-6
ISBN-13: 978-1-934159-50-7

CONTENTS

"Still, they (the Burmese) were beautiful as he had not before known beauty, and gentle and sane in their own enduring way. They were not weak people; they were only defenseless. They were stronger in their defenselessness, than the various khaki-clad people who overrun them, and then bossed them, and left them to whatever fate other khaki-clad people would deal out."

Martha Gellhorn
"For Richer or Poorer"
1958

"You cannot be humiliated or insulted unless you allow it to happen."

Pyone Pyone Tin.
Political prisoner, Insein, 1989-1991
(1947 – 2003)

FOREWORD

This is an account of the time I spent in Insein Prison, from July 20, 1989, to April 26, 1992, a period of almost one thousand days.

Less than three years is nothing when compared to the time served by other women who were in for much longer periods. It was also not so bad for me, since I had no husband or children to fret over.

Based on what has been shown in the international media, where Insein Prison is invariably portrayed as "infamous for its torture," some readers may expect an account filled with women political prisoners raped by male guards and subjected to frequent torture.

Rape by male guards or torture didn't happen to the women inmates of Insein, although I can't be certain of those who were in the hands of the Military Intelligence or the police during the uprising of 1988. That year, a young woman told the BBC she was raped in Insein but the account turned out to be untrue; she had thought that it would help the cause for democracy.

It does not matter to me if readers believe my accounts or not; they have the right to believe what they want. What disgusts me is the number of people I have met who were actually disappointed or upset that we weren't raped by the male guards.

A young student in my cellblock once asked me to tell people that I had been tortured in jail if I were released before she was, so that more pressure on the ruling regime would come from abroad. I told her that I would never do that; I wouldn't lie even for my beliefs, since the means to attain our democratic goals should be honest as well as realistic.

There was torture during interrogations by the Military Intelligence officers when the arrested person was thought to be hiding some information. Some jails such as the ones in Thayet or Tharyarwaddy were famous for harsh treatment, depending upon the personality of the chief jailer. Jails in hot and dry regions like Thayet must be like hell, I think.

However, male prisoners, if they had any connections to the Burma Communist Party or if they were ex-military, were treated harshly and were never among those released by special order—nor were women with BCP connections.

Even someone like the famous and respected editor and writer U Win Tin (member of the Central Executive Committee of the National League for Democracy and one of its founders) was treated very badly, although he was widely believed to be a leftist and not a member of the BCP.

U Win Htein, a retired military man, served two separate terms. During the second he was actually on the road on his way home after being released from a remote jail when his escorts took him back to his prison. This sort of mental torture must be devastating.

Torture was not a part of daily jail time, with prisoners being hauled out of their cells without cause just to be beaten up. However, political activities in jail were punished with severe beatings, harsher than merited. On September 25, 1990, there was a strike inside Insein and the men involved in it were very badly beaten. The prison doctor checked them periodically, only to tell the guards it was all right to carry on. Afterward, as additional punishment and humiliation, some were sent to live in the smelly and flea-ridden cells that had once been occupied by the dogs of the K-9 forces.

Five young women political prisoners participated in that September strike and afterward they were transferred to Tharyarwaddy Prison. They were beaten both after the strike was ended, and later on their way to the new prison.

In spite of these crackdowns, most political prisoners in Myanmar, men or women, whether Buddhist or Christian or of other faiths, have an amazing generosity of spirit.

In 2004 many Military Intelligence personnel were arrested on corruption charges. One MI officer, who had arrested a number of political prisoners, was sent to jail in Mandalay where his erstwhile victims were incarcerated. Expecting them to take revenge, he went in trembling with terror but to his surprise and relief they comforted him, gave him food, and taught him how to meditate. I heard he burst into tears at their welcome, is now meditating diligently, and in turn is forgiving of his captors.

Life in Insein wasn't easy, as living conditions were very primitive. Good medical care was unavailable even in the state hospitals, let alone in prison, and medication had to be sent to us from home. Fortunately, during our time none of us were seriously ill.

However, one writer/doctor, who was arrested in 1994 two years after our release by special order, had a serious gynecological problem which grew worse after she arrived in Insein. She was in constant pain and under medication. Because she was a doctor, she was allowed to have her pills on hand.

She accidentally witnessed a bribe being offered to a guard by another prisoner. The person who extended the bribe, afraid that she might be reported, decided to create mistrust between the doctor and the jailers by spreading the rumor that the doctor was going to kill herself with her prescribed medication. The authorities took away the doctor's pills, which led to many pain-filled days and nights for her. After nearly six years she was released and soon regained both her health and success in her profession. Now, she often travels or studies overseas.

By the time this prisoner was halfway through her incarceration, the elderly, uneducated guards of my time had all been retired and younger, stricter women with college degrees took their places. And now prison sentences are far longer…in the region of sixty years.

Ex-political prisoners are often asked by westerners if we didn't "demand to be released." For us, putting in a "demand" like that could be misconstrued down the line as a request or even worse, a plea, because in our language we do not have a word with the same aggressive connotations of "demand."

It is in the Myanmar nature to face all things good or bad with pride and dignity, and not to lose face by "losing it." For us, courage is shown by facing life calmly and without any display of anger. It is a weakness to allow others to humiliate us or break our spirits. I would say it's a thumbing of the nose at whatever destiny throws at us. In our culture physical courage has less value than inner strength.

What impressed me most in Insein was how political prisoners fared with high spirits, refusing to be cowed by misery. They may have been behind bars but their minds were free. They lived with a pride that left no room for self-pity. Their moral fiber came from not wanting to be an object of pity, and from this stemmed their ability to face anything with humor and tranquility.

In the "outside" world too, I see this pride and dignity in our people, especially in those who live in rural areas. They too have the fatalism, the resilience, and the humor to face hardship with equanimity. But I never saw this spirit stronger than among those who were imprisoned.

This is not the weakness of denial; this is strength of character.

A question often put to me is if I have any bitterness toward the military government.

I went into politics with my eyes open, fully aware of the consequences. My parents raised me to take responsibility for my actions and to stand by my beliefs; thus I put no blame on others nor do I have any regrets.

Another question is what changed in me after my stint in Insein. Having lived in a place with nothing to soften the bare bones of reality, I am now, more than ever, abhorrent of hypocrisy and sorely impatient with superficiality.

There are many more political prisoners, of whom I have fond memories, whose stories I have not told. It is only for the necessity of being concise that they weren't mentioned; my memories of them and our days together will never fade.

1. PRELUDE TO PRISON

In the Burmese language, getting married and going to jail are fates that are differentiated by only one word. For a Burmese woman who consults a fortune teller, that one word is a crucial one, since marriage, not a prison sentence, is what she usually has on her mind.

In 1987, a year after my divorce, a friend who reads palms looked at my hand and predicted I would soon be remarried. I wasn't keen on the idea. After the amicable divorce that released me from a restrictive fifteen-year marriage to a Burmese diplomat—nice guy—the prospect of another marital confinement wasn't an enticing fortune. I had no idea she foretold a literal prison that I would "fall into" and stay in for nearly three years.

From the time that I was fifteen years old until I was forty-two, I lived under a Socialist regime. It felt like a lifetime. I was never interested in politics but as an artist I chafed under the restrictions on publication and artistic expression. When a movement of unrest started in March 1988 I watched on the sidelines as students marched and often were shot down.

I began to feel guilty that young students were active while we adults sat by, watching. As an act of civil disobedience, I joined a group of artists who printed leaflets that we handed out. Together we created posters that were pasted all over town.

Martial law was lifted on August 22. Two days later, Daw Aung San Suu Kyi, the daughter of our Independence hero and martyr, General Aung San, appeared at the Yangon General Hospital compound and announced that she would make a public address at the Shwedagon Pagoda on August 26. When that day came, tens of thousands of people, including my artist friends and me, showed our support by sitting on a muddy field in the rain.

As soon as she appeared on the political scene, she was taken immediately into our hearts without question, as the daughter of our hero. This instant support as her father's daughter placed her in the role of our leader as well as a symbol of democracy.

I met Daw Aung San Suu Kyi face-to-face two days after her first public appearance, when I came to her with posters I had designed with another artist. (Years ago, I had seen her around for about three years at my school in Yangon, the Methodist English High School; I was a couple of years her junior and had badly wanted to meet her because I had heard she liked to draw, as I did. I never got the chance.) I offered to help her in any way that I could, and since I'm fluent in English, I was called to come in and work with her on the following day.

Before I went, I knew that I was entering dangerous waters. I sat down and asked myself if I would be able to face any difficulty, including death, without coming apart at the seams. I had to be sure I could do this so I wouldn't look a complete fool when the time came.

I knew it was very possible I would land in jail so I wrote down what to do in case this happened, asking several of my friends to look after my property. I packed a bag with clothes, soap, towels, and medicine so I would be ready for the day that I would be "pinched." I promised myself I wouldn't run and hide.

When I reported for duty early the next day, I was greeted by Ma Suu (as we older people called her, while the younger students addressed her as Aunty Suu). She told me to answer the telephone because many foreign journalists were calling, and I sat by the phone from the minute I arrived until late in the afternoon.

All of us who worked with Ma Suu were volunteers. My closest colleagues were Ko Maw (Maw Min Lwin) and Aung Aung (Aung Min Lwin), the sons of U Min Lwin, who had been General Aung San's trusted bodyguard. Both of them had known Ma Suu since they were children and were almost like her younger brothers. U Win Htein, an ex-military officer, was her assistant in political work. Ko Myint Swe, who was helping Ma Suu in her research into her father's life, and his poet wife Nwei were also part of the nucleus of her personal office. We all pitched in to do whatever was necessary.

A week after my arrival when the paperwork in her office reached a level of disarray that Ma Suu could no longer tolerate, she said I was wasting my time sitting by the phone and told me to organize the mass of paper instead. In the dining room of her house, which she used as her office and meeting room, I found piles of papers stacked on every available surface and shoved under chairs and tables. It took me a week to sort them out and file them.

As her personal assistant, I screened all letters to her apart from those from family and friends. I booked her appointments and generally looked after her, making sure she took her vitamins and ate at regular hours. When she traveled on campaign trips I went along and took care of her personal belongings, washed and ironed her clothes, and did everything that needed attention, which in Yangon even included sweeping up the cigarette butts discarded by visitors.

A large group of college students worked with Aung Aung and Ko Maw as bodyguards, although none of them carried any weapons. "All we can do in an emergency is bend down and bite people on the shins," Aung Aung sighed ruefully, but truly all they could do was form a barricade of bodies as protection—Ma Suu had told them no biting.

As the weeks went by, the military shot down demonstrators in the countryside. In Yangon hysterical crowds held public executions of people they suspected of being "spies." A military body called the State Law and Order Restoration Council (SLORC) took power on September 18, 1988, and announced there would soon be elections. The National League for Democracy (NLD) was formed a week later with Daw Aung San Suu Kyi as General Secretary.

At that point, because I am an artist with no love for office work, I told Ma Suu that, win or lose, after the elections I would no longer work as her personal assistant. I would help her informally as her eyes and ears among the ordinary people, and she agreed this would be useful.

After October, we went on campaign trips all over the country. At times we faced harassment or danger while in other places we had no problems at all—the township authorities who were the wiser type of military men would decide to "go fishing" and leave us to our devices, which meant that we would come in, make a few speeches, eat lunch, and leave quietly.

All of us, adults and students, men and women, rallied around Ma Suu, completely aware that we were headed for prison or worse. Even the youngest students never lost their cool but walked on calmly when guns were pointed at their midriffs. I never saw a single person turn and run or even lose composure.

Many of the boys and girls had cheerfully gone through the Buddhist rite of blessing the dead, the *Tharanagon* ritual normally performed over a corpse, although they were alive at the time. They said they wanted to make sure they departed this life with all necessary rituals completed, if this should happen in a hurry. Most of them became monks or nuns for a few days, ensuring, they half joked, that at least they would have that merit to take with them to the next life.

By early 1989, political tensions heightened between the NLD and the

SLORC and gradually grew worse. By Martyrs' Day on July 19, the forty-second anniversary of Ma Suu's father's death, we all knew it was only a matter of days before we would be arrested.

All political parties were invited to attend the government-sponsored ceremony but the NLD had declined. Ma Suu proposed that the NLD and its affiliate parties boycott the official annual ceremony held early in the morning and march with the public later instead, with herself at the head of the NLD column.

Everyone was excited about marching in a mass rally. The military government suspected we planned a riot but our intentions were only to pay respects at the mausoleum. However, we were worried about how to control the thousands of people who would march with us.

The student organizations and affiliate political parties were all alerted and were told which routes they should take on their march to join us. Ma Suu intended to leave her house at around 8:30 a.m. after offering the *Ah Yon Soon* dawn breakfast to monks in a ritual that she performed every month on the nineteenth to commemorate her father's death. This time she decided to offer the food not at her home, but at the nearby NLD headquarters.

I was told to stay in her office to man the phone in case of emergencies. Aung Aung and Ko Maw would be at Ma Suu's side, together with her student bodyguards.

On the morning of the planned march, one of my brothers-in-law, a high-ranking member of the Democracy Party headed by U Nu, our former prime minister, called me to come see him before I went to work. He was so insistent that I couldn't refuse. When I got to his house, I found out that he wanted to give Ma Suu and me each a tiny piece cut from a "powerful" monk's robe; he said it would keep us safe. I was deeply touched and thanked him sincerely although I do not believe in talismans.

I arrived at around 8 a.m., and about fifteen minutes later, Ma Suu arrived with Aung Aung and Ko Maw.

"We're not going out today," Aung Aung told me as Ma Suu went upstairs to her private rooms.

He said the decision had been made right after the Soon ceremony. He handed me a piece of paper that was an announcement signed by Ma Suu, urging demonstrators not to go out in the streets at all to commemorate Martyrs' Day but to remember her father privately at home. People had been sent to distribute the announcement all over town but by then it was too late to call off a march of this magnitude.

When Ma Suu came back downstairs, I gave her one of the small pieces of the monk's robe.

We heard within a few hours that almost all of the students who had marched toward the Martyrs' Mausoleum had been beaten up. By dusk we knew that while many had been arrested, most of them had climbed over walls and cut through private gardens to escape. I went home heavyhearted.

Early the next day, Aung Aung called me. "Don't come today. Things don't look too good," he said. "Soldiers are all over the road."

I told him that in that case I should be with them, and left at once. In my haste I left behind the bag I had packed for just such an occasion. It had been ready for months but when the time came I forgot all about it.

When I arrived I noticed military trucks were parked all over the street, which had very little traffic. Ma Suu told me that she had decided the night before that the only thing for her to do was to be arrested. She said that she slept well after she made this decision.

Just then, the other members of the NLD Central Executive Committee came for a meeting with her. They were all ex-military men; by then the intelligentsia members had all been arrested.

By 9 a.m., soldiers came to her gate and no one was allowed in or out; we heard that U Nu came but was turned away. The CEC members were allowed to leave around 2 p.m.

Ma Suu's two sons were visiting her at the time. The oldest, Alexander, stayed upstairs reading while Kim, who was about twelve, taught me to play Monopoly. When I got a "get out of jail free" card, I joked that I had better keep it in case I needed to use it and tucked it away in my purse.

I gave Ma Suu's younger aunt who lived in the same compound the jewelry I was wearing and my watch for safekeeping. We were all sure that before the day was out we would be in Insein Prison and I didn't want to take valuable possessions into jail.

Most of us sat and chatted with Ma Suu, laughing and joking. We all had made our choices long ago and nobody seemed the slightest bit worried by the prospect of imprisonment.

Around 4 p.m. an army officer came to the gate, asking permission to enter, and a student came running to us with the news. Ma Suu and I decided that we couldn't be arrested without wearing a dash of French perfume and she ran upstairs to put some on while I used a small bottle that I had in my bag. Then, both of us in a cloud of scent, we walked out to the gate with U Win Htein, trailed by the boys. The army officer entered, followed by personnel of the Red Cross, police, immigration, etc., and politely handed her the paper stating she was being put under Section 10 (B), house arrest.

At first we were all led to believe that we might be allowed to stay in the house with Ma Suu. All evening we were separated from her, kept inside the big bamboo hall used for meetings, some yards away from the main house where she remained. Before we were taken there, we each were asked if we were willing to be incarcerated in the house and compound with Ma Suu. Most of us said yes. Naively thinking that the offer was sincere, I asked if I could have my paints and canvases with me.

Ko Myint Swe was told to make a list of those of us who were willing to stay. But after we had waited for a long time in the hall, he picked up the list and silently tore it up, smiling at me. By then we both knew that we wouldn't be able to stay with Ma Suu, nor would we return to our own homes.

At about 9 p.m., we saw two big trucks come into the compound and park near the house. We were led outside and told to climb into them.

Before we were loaded into the trucks, I went in the house and took a plastic bag I kept near my desk that held spare clothing, a towel, tooth-brush, and sweater, since sometimes I needed to spend the night in the guest room upstairs. Ma Suu gave me a large cake of Yardley's lavender soap, a big tube of Colgate toothpaste, and an extra toothbrush. She also insisted I take her expensive leather sandals which were made for long hikes, although I protested that I doubted very much that I would be allowed to go on one. We hugged and told each other to take care.

I slung my bag into the back of the truck and climbed in. The canvas flaps closed behind us. We couldn't see out. There were no seats; we sat on the floor. Aung Aung handed me a plastic tablecloth that he had picked up as he left, whispering, "Bedbugs."

Then all of us, about thirty men and I, the only female, were driven to Insein Prison.

2. INTRODUCTION TO INSEIN

The two trucks backed up to the huge main doors of the prison, high, thick metal doors painted a deep rich scarlet. Set into them was a smaller door which opened to receive us.

The men went in first, while a woman prison guard took me in after them. The door closed behind me with a deep clang, a noise that was startling, emphasizing that a heavy metal barrier between us and the world had been shut.

The men were already in rows in the large high-ceilinged room, in the crouching position used by prisoners called *pon san*, squatting on their heels with lowered heads, hands folded on their knees. I didn't want to squat. I sat close to the floor with my back straight, balancing on my raised heels.

One of the guys peeked over his shoulder at me and wriggled his eyebrows in the direction of someone sitting at a desk. It was a young Military Intelligence officer we had encountered in April, when some of us had been briefly detained at an MI post in a lovely park, of all places. He smiled smugly as he looked at us, probably because he had not been able to browbeat us at our previous meeting and wanted to give us a "look where you are now" message.

Later, I was to meet many MI officers during interrogations, and none of them showed any sign that they were happy to have us incarcerated, even if they actually were. But this chap wasn't about to lose his chance to gloat, although his expression became somewhat forced, since we didn't look upset this time around, either.

As I was the only one of the group who wasn't male, the woman guard immediately led me into a small dusty storeroom and searched me, running her hands over my body. When I giggled she looked up in surprise, and I told her it tickled. (Later when I got to know her, she said she was amazed that someone could laugh when they were about to be imprisoned and I replied that I had been preparing myself for almost a year.)

She turned my bag upside down, removing my notebook, my keys, every scrap of paper including the "get out of jail free" Monopoly card, a few sanitary napkins, and cash. I was allowed to keep the plastic sheet Aung Aung gave me, a makeup kit, five lipsticks, and the toothbrush, toothpaste, and soap given to me at the last minute by Ma Suu. I learned later that my arrival in Insein with five lipsticks and a box of makeup had caused quite a stir.

I was unhappy that my thick, red notebook was taken away from me. In it I had sketches and poems, both my own and ones I had copied from Emily Dickinson. I never saw it again, much to my annoyance, although I pestered the MI about it at every interrogation session. I didn't think the MI officers were allowed to give back any papers they took away, even poetry, but they couldn't very well say so and every time I asked they replied politely enough that they would look for it.

I was escorted to the women's section of the jail where there was another red metal door, much smaller than the first, domed at the top, and set deep in the wall. It opened with much clanging, and I was vaguely aware of a brick bungalow just beyond the entrance. I was led through another opening on the left, this time through a high corrugated iron fence, past a two-story red brick building, again through another fence, and up the stairs of a two-story building with thick cream-colored brick walls.

I looked up to see a barred window. Among the faces peering out at me, I recognized four women from the NLD who had been arrested the day before. As the iron-barred door was unlocked and I walked in, they clustered around to hug me, whispering for news of Ma Suu. "House arrest," I whispered back. They were relieved it wasn't worse.

There were eleven of us in that huge hall. Apart from the four I already knew—Tin, Pyone, Mar, and Aye, who were about my age—there were six others: Khet, another woman of our age and five who were much younger, some of them students.

The door clanged shut, the keys jangling noisily as it was locked. We talked in whispers, apprehensive, excited, and determined not to be afraid. Dinnertime was already over but someone gave me a banana. With water from a terra-cotta pot perched on the windowsill, that was enough.

We were in a long hall, with ten barred French windows on each side. On the side of the hall that overlooked the outer wall, the doors were open to the elements, which gave a very open, airy feel to the place. With the whitewashed walls and polished wooden floors, the space looked somewhat like a ballroom in a very run-down mansion, its gleaming floors infested with bedbugs.

At the far end behind rickety plywood screens were two big, glazed jars under waist-high wooden platforms. These were the loos. A nearby barred door led to the back stairs where pairs of criminal prisoners who were assigned to loo duty carried out the jars hung on a thick yoke.

I heard taps being played. It was 9 p.m., which was bedtime but not lights out. Lights were kept on all night so that all of our actions could be seen.

I placed the piece of blue plastic under my "bedding," which was a spare *longyi* (a sarong) spread on the floor with my sweater as pillow. The plastic, large enough that I could share it with Tin, was protection from the bedbugs that were one of the worst discomforts of jail.

A shrine was placed high on the wall at our end, a simple colored print of the Buddha with a vase in front of it that held a few green leaves. We slept in two rows with our heads facing toward it, the younger girls a yard or so away from our feet. Lying with my arm on my forehead, I thought to myself that if I had to stay in this place for a week, I would surely go mad. Or die.

The four women I already knew, Pyone, Tin, Mar, and Aye, had been arrested all together for distributing leaflets telling people to stay home in protest of the official Martyrs' Day ceremony. Mar and Aye were sisters-in-law, Tin and I had been classmates in high school, and Pyone was my close friend.

Tin was slim, dark, sophisticated, and attractive, while Aye had a sweet-faced gentleness. Mar was one of the most charming women I have ever met, with a winsome prettiness and a childlike naïveté; her husband was madly in love with her. Pyone was a strong-minded, down-to-earth person with a strong sense of justice and fairness. Once you saw her steady gaze and strong jaw, you immediately knew you could trust her but couldn't mess with her.

The others were younger women, one of them caught up in the crowd while watching the protestors running hither and thither, chased by riot police. Someone rushing by had shoved his basket of flowers into her hands, and she had been happy to receive such a pretty thing. The police found her with it and she was unable to prove that she wasn't headed for the Martyrs' Mausoleum. When she was sentenced to three years, the basket, wilted flowers and all, had been produced as evidence. She said she had wanted to go over and kick the darned thing.

The next morning, we were led out to a large concrete water tank near the gate I had entered the previous night, while the other criminal prisoners downstairs were still locked in. We weren't sentenced yet, and so couldn't have any contact with sentenced prisoners. We shared one plastic bowl, soap, toothpaste, and the extra toothbrush Ma Suu had given me. Immediately afterward we were taken upstairs and locked in again while those downstairs were let out for their turn at the tank, bringing their plastic bowls with them. They had to line up along the sides; when bathing they could only use a limited amount of water, counted by each plastic bowlful scooped from the tank.

A woman guard came to the door, silently handed us a bag of biscuits, and left. We washed them down with water.

Lunch came at about 10 a.m. It was rice served on dented aluminum plates with a bowl of lentil soup for each of us. I knew I couldn't be fussy and risk health problems by not eating enough. It was my good fortune that I have never been a fussy eater; I ate everything.

We all shared a bit of pickled mango left over from yesterday's dinner. My friends had a few hard-boiled eggs from the previous day's ration, and Khet turned the eggs into a salad with a bit of oil, salt, and some MSG that a guard had given them. It was the best egg salad I ever had in my life.

The rice was coarse and dotted with husks. Fortunately, I tend to swallow without chewing so I didn't even bother to pick them out. I dashed soup onto my rice and sort of swooshed down the soupy mixture quickly. My tight schedule of the past months had taught me to eat at a fast pace.

I ate so rapidly I finished well before the others. I washed my hands and laid down on my pallet, arm on my forehead, thinking hard. I had left behind two big cupboards full of letters and papers but they weren't dangerous to anyone, including me, nothing I needed to worry about.

Dinner that evening was better than lunch. There were chunks of beef in watery gravy, and a few hard-boiled eggs for those who didn't eat beef.

That was Friday, and "meat day" in Insein was Thursday as I later discovered, so this meal was our nutritional supplement, given to nursing mothers, the elderly and infirm, and to some political prisoners. The supplement also provided hot rice gruel for breakfast each morning, which was very welcome on cold days. As the same food was given to inpatients at the prison hospital, it was called "hospital fare."

Our interrogations started that night at about 7 p.m., with all of us being taken in a truck to the Annex Jail outside of the main prison. On the truck next to me was a girl with swollen lips who had been beaten during the march on July 19.

She swayed as she sat and I gently pulled her head onto my lap. She murmured, "Is Aunty Suu all right?" I bent down and whispered that she was fine but under house arrest.

Another girl from Ma Suu's compound was on the truck, and on her recently shaved head (that remained from her recent stint in a nunnery), there was a large bump. Later, she would often joke that the wooden baton of the riot police hitting her bald head made a twanging sound that she was sure echoed for miles.

This time the huge metal front doors opened to let the truck through. In a large two-story wooden building just beyond the walls that was obviously an office, we wrote down our biographical information. We were brought back after about three hours, during which some of us sat doing nothing while others were questioned. The girl who had rested on my lap was released.

The next day Khet and I were sent to live in the *tike*, or the brick cellblock in the first courtyard. I shared my cell with four young women;

Khet was in the adjoining one with as many cellmates as I had. Attorney Daw Myint Myint Khin, a CEC member of the NLD, was already ensconced in another cell.

The first night that Khet and I stayed there, we were given—"from the Military Intelligence," as the guard told us— a small towel, a toothbrush, and a little bar of soap, the kind provided in hotel bathrooms.

Within the week the friends we had left behind in the hall were sentenced to three years each. I was told by the jailer who read us the official document that I was to be detained without charge under Section 10 (A) of the State Protection Law; I could receive food parcels every Monday but no visits. This was passed on to my large group of friends—including my ex-husband and his wife—who had been hanging around the gate of Insein Prison.

After two weeks, friends living at the same address as I but on another floor of the building were allowed to send me a food parcel plus one thin cotton blanket and a thicker one for cold nights, more clothes, a plastic drinking cup, bowl, spoons, and plate—as well as a sweater, which I gave away as I already had one.

(All households must have registration forms and the only people who could send in food to or visit any prisoners had to be on the same form, be of the immediate family, or at least live at the same address. My mother was too old to be delivering my food so my friends who lived in my building took over, for which I later compensated them handsomely.)

Our cellblock had once been an office building that was now partitioned into ten cells, with a double layer of wooden planks between each one. There were five cells on either side of a narrow central aisle. Each had a large, screened window with wooden bars on the outer wall. The wooden door in the inner wall had an opening in the top half with a double screen, which could be closed from the outside with a wooden flap. There were a couple of thick bamboo mats on the floor, which was of rough, porous concrete. Older women or those who had been there for a number of months were provided with wooden sleeping platforms four inches high. There were never enough platforms to go around; I got one only after I was the last prisoner left in the whole cellblock.

In one corner near the door was a shallow glazed-ware basin, about twenty inches wide across the rim, covered with a small square of corrugated iron. That was the loo, which was emptied and washed twice a day by the loo carriers. Next to that was a water pot for washing after using the loo, filled each day by another group, the loo water carriers. Each prison sentence came with the term "with hard labor," and these tasks were some of the work details.

These prisoners were usually the poorest among us, who requested loo duty because it gave them the maximum number of days taken off their sentences plus unlimited bath times. This disgusting job was also given to criminal prisoners as severe punishment for infringement of rules. Most of these criminals were in jail under the vagrancy law Section 30 (D) and thus they were just called Thirty D.

Nearer the inner wall was yet another pot for drinking water, along with a basin for dish water. The drinking water pot was filled and the dishwashing basin emptied by another and much cleaner group of women who had committed petty crimes. They also hauled water for our baths.

Old women who were sentenced to prison time, usually for gambling offenses, picked up cheroot butts or plastic bags in the grounds. Vagrants washed toilet basins or cleaned the outside loos of the halls. Criminals watered the vegetable gardens or scrubbed the drains with pieces of brick. I have never seen cleaner drains anywhere else.

Many picked the husks from the rice sent to us from the kitchens, before it was cooked. Some women inmates carried in the cooked rice and the soup bins which male prisoners, who worked kitchen duty, left at our gate. One pretty young political prisoner, she of the shaved head, helped at the clinic and looked after the health of children in jail. Children came into prison with their mothers when there was no one else to look after them, and babies were often born inside. This young woman gave them daily vitamins and made sure that they were kept clean.

Our cells were about nine feet by seven feet. The right-hand side of the cellblock was sunny and looked out upon a high corrugated metal fence and a strip of ground, but the left side was dark because a roofed shed extended from it. Beyond the roof was a large yard and set near the front gate was a concrete water tank where guards bathed.

In the shed right under the window of the first cell was the office, with a table and cupboards for files and a floor of packed dirt. This is where new arrivals were checked in and their records set down. Behind our block was some open space where later the prisoners planted string beans on bamboo runners. At one corner, in a space paved with concrete, there were two glazed jars of water for our baths.

At first, because I had to share my cell with four others, it was rather a tight fit. We slept on three rough bamboo mats. One young woman sang constantly, and off-key, which drove us wild. We were as happy for ourselves as we were for her when she was released.

Everyone in my cell except me was released or sentenced after about two weeks, including Khet who was sentenced to three years and moved back to the hall with our other friends. I was left alone in my cell. Perhaps some might have preferred a cellmate to keep from feeling lonely but I liked my privacy. Besides, I could easily talk to friends in other cells.

Daw Myint Myint Khin, or Ma Ma Myint as I called her, had the first cell on the right-hand row. She was my mother's lawyer, and later my own attorney after we were both released. The younger political prisoners called her Aunty Gyi or elder aunt, and I automatically became

Aunty Lay or younger aunt. Ma Ma Myint's nickname didn't stick but mine did. To this day, if I hear anyone calling me Aunty Lay in the street I can be sure it's one of us.

After I began to receive food parcels, Ma Ma Myint and I discovered that if something needed to be mixed we could do it by putting it in a plastic bag and squeezing the bag around from outside, thus keeping our fingers clean. We did this even after we regained our freedom, so everything I buy now, such as chicken salad, I mix right in the bag. I'm sure everyone in jail must have discovered this same method but Ma Ma Myint and I remain proud of our invention.

Three cells on the other side were filled with students, half of whom were released after three months, with the others sentenced to three or five years. There were empty cells, but the girls preferred not to live alone and there was a constant buzz of chatter and giggles from them. At mealtimes they took a lot of rice, because they liked to snack at odd hours of the day and night; with oil, chilies, salt, and fried dried shrimps they could make a rice salad.

Two cells were occupied with mother-daughter pairs from the Burma Communist Party. Strangely enough, each pair kept a distance from the other, and later I learned that it was because the ranks of their husbands were different. There seemed to be a strict hierarchy in the BCP.

Prison garb for the convicted was supposed to be all white— or at least as white the clothing could be after many washings. The prison issued rough homespun white clothing, but the more affluent wore new white garments made of better fabric, sent to them by their families. All of those who had received their sentences were required to wear white when their families visited and on the days when the senior male jailers made their weekly rounds.. After those occasions, most prisoners changed back into whatever clothing they had been sent from home, while the poorest changed into the clothes they had on their backs when they first arrived.

As I wasn't sentenced at the time I wasn't required to wear white, but since I couldn't get enough clothes sent to me I wore the prison uniform constantly. But I was always given the newer pieces of convict garments, the guards rolling their eyes in horror that a detainee would want to wear the "inauspicious" prison garb. However, being dressed in white made me feel clean and fresh and the cotton was very cool. In fact, the only person who wore convict whites every day was me, the unsentenced woman who had no right to wear them.

I wasn't allowed to communicate with anyone outside so at first, although I received food parcels I couldn't ask for specific items. Only after jailer Daw Aye Aye Than took over our section was I allowed to have her write down what I wanted my friends to send me.

At our meals those who could afford it used melamine plates sent from home. I was given the usual prison ware, an aluminum plate and a bowl, both a bit battered and black with grime. With some clean sand gathered from the grounds, I scrubbed them until they shone like polished silver. It was a comfort to me to have a sparkling clean plate although I ate coarse rice from it. Throughout my prison years I kept my plate and bowl sparkling, especially after a friendly guard got me some scouring pads.

As soon as I began to live alone, I set about keeping my cell as clean as possible. I scrubbed the floor with water and a swath of coconut husk a guard gave me. Because the concrete was porous, I didn't even need to mop it; the water simply seeped away. That was convenient; during hot summers I could pour water on the floor and keep my cell cool.

I was among the earliest to be arrested so after Ma Ma Myint and others were released and I was alone in my cellblock, I received a four-inch-high wooden platform. Over this I laid my plastic sheet and then all of my longyi to make a mattress. My sweater wrapped in a towel was my pillow since mattresses, pillows, or mosquito nets weren't allowed in prison.

Lights were kept on even during the day, except in the height of summer when they added to the heat. This was so any infringement of the rules could be spotted. Lack of visibility was also why mosquito nets weren't allowed, the guards told me.

I needed to block the light that shone in my eyes so I unraveled a sleeve of my sweater to make a clothesline. At a strategic place I hung my handkerchief and with its shadow falling right on my face, I could at last sleep for the whole night. Fortunately I always lie very still while sleeping.

Every prisoner had the right to a prison blanket of rough woven white cotton with a red stripe on each side. After many washes the blanket became very soft. There weren't enough for everyone but we prisoners in the cells got one each. I used mine as my bedspread and was happy to see my bed so white and neat.

When later more inmates came to the cellblock with not enough wooden platforms to go around, one jailer, Daw Aye Aye Than, was kind enough to give each room several bamboo mats so that they could be stacked as added protection against the cold floor. We believed that the coldness of concrete was more dangerous to muscles and nerves than anything else, so this was a great addition to our cells.

The door to our cellblock was directly in line with the red metal front door that led to the whole section. It clanged loudly each time it was opened and when I heard that sound at night my heart would always jump. Perhaps, I thought, it meant that more of my colleagues had been brought here—political prisoners usually arrived after closing hours.

I longed to paint the red door, domed and set deep in the thick walls with a small green plant growing wild by its edge. Every time I paced along the middle aisle on my exercise outing I would stare at the door, memorizing it for fifteen minutes a day.

I vowed to paint it one day and months after my release, I did. But as soon as I picked up my brush, my hand shook uncontrollably and my heart jumped wildly in my chest. I was horrified. It took me an hour to calm down and try again. When the painting was finished, it had none of the careful brushstrokes that I usually use in my artwork.

3. INTERROGATIONS

When we were taken out for interrogations, we were led to the Military
Intelligence compound next to the Main Jail offices with hoods over our
heads. This was standard procedure, so we couldn't be identified by any
prisoners passing by and couldn't see our surroundings.

My hood was sewn out of blue cotton, with a double thickness over the
face. It fell just below my jawline, and I was able to see a few feet in front
of me. It wasn't suffocating unless the hood was unwashed and musty.

Sometimes when there were more people to be interrogated than usual
and not enough hoods, the inmates would be lined up with a cotton
blanket spread over their heads. The young girls, if they had to walk
in this manner, would clutch one another's waist as if they were line
dancing. They played at being a train, calling out "Toot-toot," until the
harassed guards begged the girls to please stop this noise, they'd be fired
if they led a train through the offices.

Once I was escorted, hood over my head, to an interrogation session by
a guard who disliked "undignified behavior," an elderly, stick-thin, coal-
dark country woman whom everyone called Mother Kyi. She was always
harping about the "proper dignity of women" when the girls played the
fool, and was perpetually in a nervous state with us.

She held my arm to guide me as we slowly ambled along the path, although under the edge of my hood, I could see the ground about three feet in front of me. To tease her I led her, as if blindly, toward the drain by the road while she clutched my arm and dragged me back, screeching in alarm, "Watch out! Watch out! You're heading for a ditch! Hold on to me!" I knew she wouldn't dare scold me in front of the male guards in the offices and the prisoners around us. Besides, she had no idea I could see.

When we got back to our place, with me again "blindly" heading toward the drains on the way, she asked the jailer if she could be excused from taking any of us political prisoners to interrogation sessions again. To her dismay and our delight, the jailer said sharply that if she happened to be on duty and it was her turn, she had to do it. As it happened, poor Mother Kyi was almost always on duty when any of us needed "to go."

Once when a new young guard escorting me had no idea where the interrogations took place, I was the one to give her directions by peering out under the rim of the hood at the road I had so often walked. We both thought this was hilarious.

The interrogating rooms I was taken to in Insein were in one brick building in a compound just beyond the Main Jail offices. A corridor that had entrances at each end ran in the middle of this block, with two rooms on either side. The walls were painted a cream color, dingy in places, with a concrete floor, a 40-watt tube light attached to the ceiling, and a wooden desk which had a wooden chair on either side. Another chair where the woman guard sat was by the door, kept opened for ventilation purposes; on the outer wall of each room was a window, which was kept closed. (When women were interrogated in Insein, a woman guard was always present in the room.)

I had almost nothing to hide from my interrogators because I had worked alone. My office work was pretty straightforward; I made appointments, typed letters, and filed reports. Mostly these were long verses of poetry in loving homage to Daw Aung San Suu Kyi, complaints about other party members, accounting reports, or simple expressions of good wishes. Nevertheless my files filled two cupboards and the MI had to go through every page. For the first six months that I was in prison, I was interrogated on the average of three times a week.

Through my interrogation periods, I met about a dozen Military Intelligence officers who asked the same questions over and over again, probably to make sure I wasn't lying. Since there was nothing I needed to hide and because I possess the memory of an elephant, the repetitions just made me very sleepy. At least I didn't doze off with my head on the desk, as one of the girls did.

She was from our cellblock, a slender student majoring in physics who liked to sleep and snore, although, praise be, not too loudly. Once she came back in the morning after an all-night session. She passed my door when I was looking out through the screened opening, and I asked sympathetically if she had slept at all. She said yes indeed she did; at about midnight she had told the officer she would like a nap and put her head down on the desk. She woke up in the morning just in time to be sent back to her cell.

Poor Mother Kyi who was with her all night hissed her complaint to me, that the girl had snored, and that it was "a disgrace for young girls to snore in front of strange men." And then she had to sit and listen to the snores without being allowed to nap herself. "You political prisoners are all such nuisances," she wailed after locking the girl in her cell. "I should die soon or you all should be freed, one thing or the other."

I could imagine the nonplussed MI staring in disbelief when our young friend fell into a deep sleep as soon as she put down her head. Maybe he too needed rest. The interrogators weren't as numerous as the interrogatees, and by the third month they began to look haggard, with dark rings under their eyes and blotchy complexions. One youngish chap— you could never find out their names, they wouldn't tell you if you asked—had acne breaking out all over his face when I last saw him.

In December of 1989 we heard rumors that our group might be released very soon. All of us, men and women, went for short interrogations almost at the same time and the usual rooms were all full. With hoods or blankets on our heads we couldn't see which of our male colleagues were there but I recognized a pair of slender, dark feet that I was sure belonged to my friend Ko Myint Swe.

That day happened to be my birthday and since I wasn't told I would be interrogated that morning, as soon as I got up I had put on makeup with a lavish hand, pink cheeks, green eyelids and all. The MI officer, the poor young man with acne, looked dumbfounded when I removed my hood with a flourish and showed him my face painted in its many hues.

When I told him it was my birthday, he understood the reason for the makeup but he didn't wish me a happy birthday—I doubt if interrogation officers were allowed to show that much civility. Just to pay him back, I took the cap Mother Kyi had taken off to fan herself with and plopped it on my head. He couldn't help but burst into laughter while Mother Kyi and I stared stone-faced at him. He did however hint that we might be released soon. Although we weren't, almost all interrogation sessions ceased from that point.

One question that was repeatedly put to me early on was, "Who had persuaded you to join the movement?" I think they were trying to get me to name names and blame others.

Since I have been a decisive and strong-minded person from childhood, I resented the implication that someone else coerced me to be involved in politics. I always replied that I had seen the young students marching and had felt guilty that we adults were watching from the sidelines. I told them I went to join my artist group because I wanted freedom of expression. As a painter I needed to be able to paint without fear of censorship, and freedom of publication meant there would be some control over corruption no matter what government we might get.

So that they wouldn't twist my words, I also told them firmly that I didn't believe freedom of publication included pornography. Taking this chance to put forth my views, I would explain all of this to my interrogators at length each time I was asked that question. After a few times they stopped asking me that particular question, probably because they had to take down every word I uttered, repetitious or not, and type it up in triplicate. (There were no computers at that time.)

Many interrogated prisoners refused to divulge anything that would hurt their colleagues. Those who told all were usually people on the fringes who weren't deeply committed to the cause. They often—incorrectly—thought that the more names they could name, the lighter would be their sentence, and they would drag in the names of acquaintances or even friends who knew little or nothing about what happened in that particular case.

The MI, convinced that the people who had been named must know something, would arrest those who had been falsely accused and press them for more information. Sometimes the process became brutal; the victims couldn't say anything even if they wanted to, because they knew nothing. The MI thought they must be hiding something of importance, because they seemed so stubbornly silent. The vicious circle would continue with the hapless person quite ignorant of what he or she was supposed to know.

Men were often battered if they were connected to the Burma Communist Party, just for the hell of it. Ever since we gained independence from the British in 1948, those who governed our country were bitter enemies with the Communists until the insurgent Communists of the BCP were finally vanquished in 1989. However, many true believers remained all over Myanmar, especially in the big cities, although they didn't openly declare their ideological orientation.

Once I was interrogated all night long. This ploy was intentional; MI thought I would be broken and become a total wreck. But as I had often stayed up quite late to paint or read or listen to music, I was fine with lack of sleep. By morning the two chaps who had been talking to me, both obviously of low rank, looked thoroughly exhausted. At 7:30 a.m., they told me, as if they were doing me a favor, that I could go back to rest in my cell. I said, "No, no, it's fine, I'm not at all sleepy, please carry on." They stared at me in horror and I never faced another all-nighter again. I was able to go to bed once I was back in my cell but they had to go straight to work.

During the long (about four hours) or short (an hour) interrogation sessions over the months, my mind was apt to wander. I would remember my Lost Red Book and the poetry it contained, and would recite a few verses just to let my interrogators know how important my book was to me. They didn't like the interruptions nor did they seem to appreciate poetry and would firmly put me back on track. But after a few minutes, I couldn't help telling them yet again how much I liked Emily Dickinson. I believe I might have bred a deep, lifelong dislike for poetry in a few military hearts.

When I was given a paper and pen to put down my thoughts, I was so thrilled to have them that I would start to draw, something I missed badly. Although my sketches weren't bad, they weren't appreciated and papers and pens no longer came my way.

I got so bored with the repeated questions that after the second session I began to try to bring something back from those meetings. Sometimes I returned to my cell with a nail I found in the dust in the corner of the room (useful to hang up plastic bags), sometimes a stick broken off from the handle of a broom (inserted into the crack of a wall it made a peg), and once a real treasure—a piece of tin to use as a knife to cut vegetables. The others would wait to see what I would bring back and I found it a challenge to steal something, anything, useful or not.

Once, the interrogator left the room and forgot his bag on the table; out of it peeked the end of a purple plastic comb. I never wanted anything more than I wanted that comb, but thought that later, if he also mis-placed his cash, the theft would come down on my head. So to console myself I unscrewed the bolt of my folding chair and returned with that instead. I hoped the next person to sit on that chair wouldn't fall over, but it was a prize, although utterly useless. "The last of the stolen goods," I announced to my cellblock mates. "I will give up this life of crime and steal no more."

Frankly, I was getting desperate trying to find anything that wasn't bolted down and was small enough to hide in my underwear.

Sometimes the interrogators didn't question me but talked about their plans for the country, such as for the upcoming elections which were to be held in May 1990. Once or twice I was blindfolded during a session, but as I wasn't hurt in any way the blindfold wasn't intimidating.

One officer said something to me while I was blindfolded that stuck in my mind. About a year later, without a blindfold, I was being "talked to" by a young officer I had never seen before, who in the course of lecturing me said, "As I told you once before..." and repeated what I had heard with a blindfold on. Immediately I said to him, "Aha! So that was you when I was blindfo—"

Before I finished my sentence he hurriedly said, "Never mind that! Never mind!" And he ended his talk as quickly as he could.

A few weeks after my arrival, I was taken to a large hall to watch a videotaped meeting of the Executive Committee members of the Burma Communist Party. There I saw all the men whom I had not seen since we arrived in Insein together. I had to sit in the front row but couldn't help turning to look back at them to exchange grins, although we weren't allowed to talk. Their hair was long, some had scraggly beards, and when they saw that I had kept my short hair trimmed, they all looked amazed.

Tiger, the chap who had not only loaned his car but also drove it for Daw Aung San Suu Kyi, immediately mimed a question of how I had done it, since we weren't allowed sharp objects in prison. I mimed back how I twisted a few hairs until they became a stiff clump, and then used my nail clippers to cut them off. (It took a great deal of time, but then I had a lot of that on my hands. Almost three years later I emerged from prison with my hair as short as when I went in.)

We were shown a video taken at the meeting of the Politburo of the Burma Communist Party, way out in their jungle headquarters on the border with China. I was more interested in seeing my colleagues, but I do remember being startled when I heard one BCP top-ranker say that they should not use their party's name or the word communism in the political cause, as people wanted nothing to do with Communism.

How true, I thought, we have had it up to there with twenty-six years of Socialism and anything redder than that was considered alarming if not downright disgusting. I was getting to know the BCP members in my cellblock, highly intelligent, disciplined, dedicated, and committed people who leaned more toward Chinese ideology than Russian. Much as I liked them, I hated their policy.

When China began to think that making money was glorious, the BCP members were very hurt and disappointed at this betrayal. No one was more appalled than they when the Chinese Communists began appearing in magazines or on TV, no longer in dark grimy blue pajamas, but wearing miniskirts and stilettos or pale blue silk suits with wide lapels.

About a year after we saw the BCP meeting video, I was again taken by a guard to watch a movie based on the 1988 uprising. I was more eager to see my colleagues than to watch a propaganda movie but most of them weren't present, as they had attended an earlier show. The men in the audience were almost all strangers to me.

One of them was a sweet-faced, elderly gentleman, actually a prince of royal blood, a grandson of our last king. Everyone called him Taw Taw, a shortened version of his very regal name. He sat next to me holding a small bag of biscuits "to settle my stomach." Leaning toward the Left and nicknamed the Red Prince, he had no interest in being the legal heir to the throne of Myanmar, although he had the right to the title.

As the movie unfolded and the leading lady came into view with tons of makeup on her face, he remarked, "My, my, it's been so long since I've seen a pretty woman!"

The young men sitting behind him cried, "Oh, Grandpa Taw, spare us some pity!" and all of us cracked up. As a colleague, I wasn't considered a woman, and it is an undeniable fact that I could never be called pretty. Jokes flew around the room as we ignored the movie and whispered to each other.

Sometime in late 1991, I was taken out without a blindfold by car, to see an exhibition called "The Atrocities of 1988." I was happy to see the outside world and to view the Shwedagon Pagoda in all its glory. There were new concrete flower boxes along the middle of Pyay Road painted a cheerful, bright turquoise lined with pink. It was a sight that grated on me as I have a fragile sensitivity to colors.

I begged my accompanying intelligence man to please tell the authorities responsible for this project that using turquoise and bright pink on public works made a most annoying combination. He merely grunted; I am not sure MI personnel care much for colors one way or the other.

At the exhibition, the photos of bloody heads with staring dead eyes lying in rows freaked me out so much that I asked to be taken back and to this day remember little of what I saw. I only remember seeing Ko Myint Swe in the distance in the large hall, his hair curling to his shoulders, his frame as thin as ever. I thought of his poet wife Nwei, with her lilting, pretty way of talking, and how it was "darling" all the time as they talked together so I had taken to calling them U Darling and Daw Darling.

How they must miss each other, I thought.

Once in the hot month of March, for five nights and six days I was taken to an outside interrogation camp on Pyay Road. I thought when I was called that it would be just another session in jail and went out after changing my clothes. I was blindfolded in the car so that I wouldn't know where I was being taken, but soon after I arrived I heard jumbo jets from the nearby international airport taking off and landing so I knew exactly where I was and in which camp. Not only that, when my blindfold was removed and I had been placed in a small office room with a desk and two chairs, I saw stenciled on the furniture: "Property of Camp 6." So much for blindfolds.

The interrogation wasn't really intense, difficult, or different, but apart from a long narrow bench, there was no place to sleep. I slept on the bench "just like a crocodile," I told myself grimly, lying straight as a rod. I was lucky that I seldom move when I sleep or else I would have fallen to the floor.

During these interrogations, one woman or another was always present. When I asked they told me that they were the wives of privates who had quarters in the compound. I sometimes heard their children shouting while they played.

Every morning a cup of weak tea and a slice of bread and butter came for my breakfast. At about 11 a.m. a lunch of rice and curry arrived, and dinner with a different curry was served at twilight. A cup of tea again came before I slept. The tea was so weak and milky I am still unsure if it was tea or some other beverage. The food was cooked and brought in by a couple of young soldiers who worried that I ate too little. "I'm dieting," I joked, but actually the fish curry of that very first meal had been a bit spicy, and I cannot eat chili in any form.

When the soldiers heard me making snuffling noises over the hot food, I heard them hissing at each other: "You put in too much chili!"

"I didn't! You did!" The food was less spicy after that, but still cooked none too well. They apologized, saying they were on kitchen detail as a punishment.

The door had glass on its upper half, painted white on the outside so that I couldn't see out. The paint was carelessly applied so there were holes that I could peek through, but all I could see was just a large paved area and more buildings with closed doors.

When I asked, I was taken out to the toilet. I think they would have allowed me to bathe or given me a toothbrush if I requested but I stubbornly refused to ask for anything apart from my necessary trips to the loo.

By the third day, I was stinking like a rotten fish: unwashed, teeth unbrushed, and closed up in a small, humid office. Wrapped as I was in my own cocoon of heady perfume, I couldn't smell myself but I noticed that anyone coming in instantly turned green. Besides, the leather sandals on my feet, the ones Ma Suu gave me, were wafting their own organic odors to add to the already piquant aroma.

At midnight of the fourth day, I was awakened for a surprise interrogation session, this time by a young officer who was freshly showered, smelling of soap and with his hair still wet. All rightee, I thought, you think I'm going to feel embarrassed just because you show up all fresh and clean while I smell like a pig?

I stared down my nose at him but didn't show how annoyed I was that he, young enough to be my son, thought he could intimidate me just by being cleaner than I and by getting me up at midnight, for God's sake.

He had a stern look on his face and began questioning me in an obviously put-on angry tone. I realized he was playing bad cop so I answered him coolly. However, I began to simmer inside. You young chump, I thought, don't you mess with me.

Finally he asked a question which was so idiotic that I exploded. He was just pretending anger but I was seriously furious. I leaped to my feet, towered over him, and thumping the tabletop with both hands to emphasize each word, answered his question slowly from between gritted teeth.

He turned pale and leaned back in his chair because I look homicidal when I'm angry. Besides, I smelled really bad. I sat down, satisfied; he turned civil and left soon afterward. The soldier's wife who had been sitting at the door as my chaperone tottered after him into the night and I went back to sleep.

By the fifth day, my interrogators seemed to be at the point of gagging when they entered the room, and I think they were happy when I was sent back to Insein the next day. I could hear the relief in their voices as I was led, blindfolded, to the car.

I arrived late in the evening, well past closing time in Insein, but the jailer and guards hurriedly held their noses and told me to please go take a bath. A Thirty D was unlocked from her hall and brought over to fill the water jars. My friends and even the guards all thought I had been freed, as I had been handed over to the MI without any comment on where I was to be taken. They were both sorry and happy to see me back, but happier still after I took a long bath, scrubbing well with what was left of Ma Suu's lavender soap.

4. DAILY LIFE

Almost all the Myanmar prisons, including Insein, are legacies of British rule. The buildings and facilities, or the lack thereof, are all the originals and prisons are still administered according to the Jail Manual of the British.

Insein Prison was shaped like an old-fashioned wall clock with a round face and a rectangular attachment where the pendulum swings. The main gate was at twelve o'clock. Our section for the convicted *A-kya* plus our one cellblock was located at about eleven o'clock. Another women's section called *A-chote*, with two cellblocks for political prisoners in that compound, was at one o'clock. This section was for women inmates not yet sentenced who were still facing one or more charges.

In the exact center was the circular area of the Main Jail, as we called the offices. All sections fanned out from that like slices of a cake. There were the warehouses and hospital, kitchens, two-story halls for criminals, and long, low rows of cells for political prisoners. At the far end inside the pendulum were the factories where prisoners made slippers, braided rope from strands of coconut husks, wove blankets or white cotton cloth for prisoners' uniforms, or practiced the craft of blacksmithing. Beyond the walls were farms, where more vegetables were grown and pigs and chickens were raised for the Thursday meat rations. Prisoners going out to work at the farms were under guard and shackled, but most of them liked to be beyond the black walls. Only the best-behaved prisoners were chosen for this.

All the halls in Insein were two-story. The men's were sectioned off into separate rooms with iron bars, while the women's halls weren't partitioned.

Near the Main Jail was a large compound, once used during British days as a juvenile facility. It housed the MI office for interrogations, a few maximum-security cells, and a small white pagoda. Farther inside there were wooden houses built on stilts, about seven, I think, each inside a compound walled with high sheets of corrugated metal. These were the houses for VIP inmates. (There were two other VIP detention centers we only knew of as *Yay Kyi Eing*, and *Ye Mon*, both apparently miles away from Yangon and in wooded and secluded areas. I believe the "bungalows" there were more comfortable than these wooden houses in Insein and the food was better too.)

Just at the entrance to the Main Jail was a very high pillar with a Buddha image on its top. Inmates and guards alike believed that if a released prisoner looked back at this pillar, that person would come in as a prisoner again. Guards escorting us on our way to freedom would nag us all the while as we walked out, "Don't look back, now…don't look back." As I had not noticed it when I came in at night and was constantly warned not to look on my way out, I now have no idea what it looked like.

All prisoners were sentenced to serve time "with hard labor." It was up to the jailers to decide who would perform which hard labor. Those of us in the cells were exempt from work, although my political friends in the halls crocheted tablecloths and curtains for various offices. It helped them pass the time—as I discovered, idle hands could nearly drive one insane. (Pyone, however, refused to do anything. She said she had worked enough in the outside world and was determined to enjoy her prison leisure, and she did.)

All labor earned points for days to be taken from each year of a sentence and for long-timers, it could accumulate into an early release years ahead of time. For example, because of the crocheting they did, my friends of Category A who had been sentenced to three years with hard labor were released after about two years and five months. Pyone, with her refusal to pick up a crochet needle, also received a sentence reduction but was released a few days later than the others.

During my time all female political prisoners were in Category A, unless they had connections to the Burma Communist Party. Petty criminals were often sent to work at rock quarries in the center of Myanmar and up-country, or on chain gangs who worked on roads. There they earned Category A status as well as a bit of extra food and cheroots. Political prisoners were never sent there; the security was too lax.

Criminal or vagrant inmates who did the dirty loo duties were in Category A. For emptying the loo pots, they earned cheroots as a tip which they used to buy special food, sausages or bananas, from other inmates.

Reveille was at 5 a.m. Taps was nice, but reveille, we all decided, was like the background music for an animated cartoon. Besides, we would hate any music that got us up at five in the morning.

Then we had to sit up in our cells or in rows in the halls for the morning head count.

The total head counts from all over the prison had to tally with the accounts at the Main Jail of the prisoners who had been released or sent elsewhere balanced with new arrivals. There might be late arrivals from the courts or emergency entries of political prisoners at night so a head count was necessary every evening and morning.

Sometimes a guard would persistently be deluded into "seeing" more inmates than there actually were, and would give the wrong count. Then the total wouldn't tally, which meant that the doors of the cell houses or halls remained locked. Guards couldn't go home after their shift, while inmates were made to sit in rows again and again to be recounted.

Sometimes it was a genuine mistake, which meant that the second count would be correct. At other times, the guards swore they had actually seen people sitting there and counted them in, when it turned out later that their eyes had deceived them…or was the mistake caused by something supernatural?

Once, for three straight days during a wet monsoon month, the count didn't tally, and no one knew how many times the whole prisoner population was counted. None of the jailers and guards were allowed to go home at the ends of their shifts and the prisoners had to sit for several recounts. Finally on the evening of the third day the count tallied; apparently in one men's hall the jailer had seen three men, heads bowed, sitting far at the back at the end of a row, who disappeared into thin air before that final count. The men sitting next to them had not seen or sensed them. The ghosts must have had a good laugh over the chaos they had created.

Fortunately the guards had counted more than the recorded number of prisoners—not as bad as a count of fewer, which would have meant a suspected breakout. Then God knows how long the jail would have been in an uproar. At least the ghosts weren't that sadistic.

People in jail are extremely superstitious. We believe that if a lock is deliberately rattled, more inmates will come in. If bunches of keys are accidentally dropped, more will be released…but it must be an accident, not deliberate. If geckoes chatter a lot in the night, it means freedom for some lucky prisoners. Everyone believes in ghosts, omens, and dreams more than they did outside. I know I did.

One incorrect head count incident was the result not of ghostly pranks but of a prisoner who, immediately after arriving, bribed a guard at the main door, then borrowed his jacket, and somehow slipped out as a large group was being admitted. For one whole day the guards all over Insein were busy counting heads again and again.

Meanwhile rumors flew outside, initiated by some families who came for a visit that day but weren't allowed to see their inmate family members. They heard from someone that a political prisoner had escaped from Insein. As usual when this sort of thing occurred, we inside weren't allowed out except to bathe, so we sat in our cells or halls and chatted to each other with no idea of what was going on. I don't remember if the fugitive was caught but the bribed guard was fired.

(Only after my release did I learn that my friends—including my ex-husband and his wife—had heard it was I who had climbed over the walls with superhuman strength, then ran "into the forest," of which there are none, and never have been, around Insein. They also heard that I was being hunted down by dogs, of which there are also none anymore. Sick with worry, my nearest and dearest in teams of twos and threes had gone off in different directions to look for me.

When we finally met face-to-face after my release, the first thing they asked was if I had been bitten by the dogs that had pursued me. Then the whole story came out. All that time I was probably making tatted lace, eating lemon barley sweets, and exchanging jokes with those in the next cell. When I heard this story I laughed so hard that I think they were somewhat miffed. Then they clammed up, refusing to give me details about where exactly they had looked, because I teased them about looking under bushes and climbing trees to peer out over the "wilderness." I still do not know where they searched; they had been desperately worried about me.)

After the inmates were up and counted, and before the doors were unlocked, those in the hall repeated a Buddhist prayer in unison, sentence by sentence, as it was said out loud by someone who had been chosen to recite. To be selected as the prayer leader was considered prestigious and it was a highly sought-after role. Non-Buddhists didn't join in but sat in place, saying their own prayers silently.

After that, everyone bathed downstairs at the tank. Vagrant prisoners then carried off the large glazed pots that had been used as loos during the night, and finally the hall doors were unlocked, staying open until 5 p.m.

There was a compound with a few trees around the hall building, and a row of toilets at the back. One large concrete water tank used for washing and bathing sat against one fence. Downstairs in the far hall was the clinic.

The hall inmates then did whatever work they needed to do, crocheting or helping the nurse in the clinic, while the criminals carried water, tended the vegetable beds, or scrubbed the drains. Those of us kept in cells didn't need to work even if we had been sentenced "with hard labor"; work involved dealing with other inmates, which was technically not allowed for those in cells.

The authorities obtained machinery from the Social Welfare Department that inmates used to make cloth flowers, and many were produced in Insein and sold at Social Welfare retail outlets. Earlier there used to be handlooms for weaving rough cotton cloth, which some women became quite skilled at, but later the looms were moved to the men's side when space was needed for more female inmates.

For health care, there was a hospital for men, and for the women a clinic run by a guard who had medical training as a health assistant. Outside hospitals had little enough medicine; the prison clinic had even less. Wealthy prisoners donated what they could for those in need; Tin gave a lot. Serious cases were sent out to Yangon General Hospital, or to Insein Hospital, under the supervision of a watchful guard. Prisoners who had to stay in these hospitals were kept in guarded wards.

The young political prisoner working in the clinic gave vitamins to the children while telling them stories, and she was always trailed by a crowd of adoring toddlers.

Many of the younger and more agile inmates polished the wooden floors, squatting in rows and using small empty bottles made of thick glass to rub against the floor as they moved forward. It made a loud racket that I couldn't identify when I first heard it in my cell; it sounded like thunder. This way of polishing really does the trick, I found, when I tried it out at my home after my release.

Living conditions in Insein were primitive and sometimes unhealthy, especially for the elderly. When prisoners couldn't get enough mats or a wooden platform to protect themselves against the cold cement floor, they suffered from aching joints or even paralysis. The lack of fresh vegetables in our diet increased health problems and some prisoners in crowded halls, especially the men, became infected with tuberculosis. Men in smaller prisons all over the country had a much harder time as facilities were few, the weather harsh, and if the jailer in charge happened to be a mean bastard, they faced rough times.

Sometimes families couldn't easily make visits if this involved long and expensive travel. That particular hardship was removed when the International Committee of the Red Cross helped by giving airfare to families for prison visits where train or road travel was difficult. To quote a friend from Myitkyina Prison who wrote to me, "Only those who have been on family visits to far-flung locations can fully appreciate the kindness and thoughtfulness of the ICRC, which pays for the airfare. And there are exiled activists who vehemently opposed the ICRC coming to this country."

In summer, there wasn't enough water and each of us could only bathe with a limited number of scoops from our bowls. We in the cells bathed from two large jars filled for us by prisoners who hauled the water from the tank. They usually felt very sorry that we were cooped up in cells, so they would bring us an extra pail or two. One jailer, Daw Khin Mya, tried to restrict our bath water but Daw Myint Myint Khin soon put an end to that by complaining to the senior jailers when they came on their Tuesday rounds.

Bathing anywhere in Myanmar, apart from the homes of the western-ized ultrarich, is not a matter of soaking in tubs. We bathe in the open, removing all clothes apart from longyi which we tuck up to cover ourselves from our breasts to below our knees, and then we pour water over our wrapped bodies. In Insein there were no showers. On our side of the prison, we all bathed in the open, under the sun.

All those facing charges were taken out in Blue—not Black—Marias on their appointed court dates. They got weekly visits and parcels from their families, as well as the chance to see their relatives while they were in court. They had to go out barefoot, ever since the time that some men escaped from a truck with the help of a file hidden in the sole of one of their slippers.

During fortnightly visits from their immediate families, prisoners walked in double file to a room near the main gate. There they were separated from their families by two screens set about a foot apart. Usu-ally the room where the family stood was packed, and shouting to each other was essential when surrounded by the noise of many people in conversation. Visits lasted about fifteen minutes; the family could bring in a food parcel, as well as cigarettes. Some political prisoners could meet their families in more private conditions, but they were separated by a double wire screen, with a guard noting down everything they said. U Win Htein's wife told me that her youngest daughter, at the time about five, would poke her tiny forefinger through a hole in the screen for her father to touch with his fingertip on the other side.

Cheroots and cigarettes had to be purchased from the official jail shop outside the gates, for it was easy to smuggle drugs in them. For the same reason, plantains were available only at the official prison store. Many of us didn't smoke the cheroots but gave them away as tips to those who carried out our loo basins and did other chores.

Food allowances in our packages from home weren't too varied: a bunch of plantains, palm sugar, instant noodles, deep fried meat or fish, a chili-dried shrimp fry called *nga pi kyaw*, cookies, sweets, milk powder, sugar, fried sausages, and other things that would keep. For immediate consumption there were fresh-cooked curries or stir-fried vegetables. At first we weren't permitted to have fresh fruits and vegetables; these had been forbidden after some people had eaten too many overripe mangoes and then suffered serious diarrhea as a result. Later we got a woman doctor who, insisting that her charges must have fresh fruit and vegetables, signed permission slips for anyone who wanted them.

If there were outbreaks of diarrhea, officials simply asked what the afflicted ones had eaten and then banned that item for a month or two, not taking into consideration that the same type of food coming in was cooked in hundreds of different kitchens. So we made sure that no sick person said she had eaten something we all liked, such as pickled tea leaves or fried roselle leaves or stewed eggplant. Everyone with a tummy upset was told to say that she had eaten only the prison fare.

When I needed something from my friends outside there was no way I could pass a message, apart from asking those who were released to call my friends for me, or to give a message to someone from our cellblock who had been sentenced and moved to the hall, so she could tell her family during a visit. This I rarely did except for things I urgently needed because I didn't want anybody to waste time on me. Besides, my friends outside kept me supplied with essential things like lemon barley sweets, prickly heat powder, and *thanakha*, the traditional bark paste that is so cooling to our faces.

But once when I needed a pair of plastic flip-flops to wear at bath-time, I sent a message through someone from our cellblock who had been moved to the hall. After the message was passed through various friends, what finally arrived was a king-sized bedsheet. It was a huge joke among my friends and the guards that Aunty Lay was thinking of getting married. It was very useful, however, since when it was folded several times over it made a nice futon.

Every Thursday was meat ration day and in the afternoon every prisoner was given a bit of boiled pork, beef, fried fish, or two hard-boiled eggs. About two years into my stay, probably due to budget cuts, the chunks of meat and fish got smaller and instead of beef, we were given an egg.

Every Saturday each inmate was offered a thin slice of yellow laundry soap and a teaspoonful of oil, but only the poorest prisoners accepted this.

On special days such as Independence, Union Day, or the religious holidays on the full moon days of *Tabaung* (March), *Waso* (July), or *Thadingyut* (October), a festive lentil soup with vegetables and spices was served. It was watery, with a few pieces of eggplant, radish, potato, and spinach, but we always looked forward to it, since it was a change in our deadly boring routine.

Every Tuesday the senior men jailers made the rounds of the cellblocks and the halls, to hear requests from prisoners about living conditions. Complaints or requests that were beyond the jurisdiction of our own jailers were made during these rounds. Because of them we received daily hot water and the services of a lady doctor and nurses.

Every morning we in the cells and the political prisoners in the halls, along with nursing mothers, children, the sick, and the elderly, were given hot, watery rice gruel for breakfast. A prisoner in charge of food would come around our cells with a bucket of this, accompanied by a guard to unlock each door. We would be locked up again until bathtime, which came about two hours later. In our cells we washed our faces, brushed our teeth, and then (in earlier days extremely awkwardly), tried to do the dirty business over the loo basin while squatting balanced on one heel, with the other leg outstretched. That was the best position.

Then we would wash our hands and eat our gruel. If we were lucky we would have milk powder and sugar to add to it; otherwise we would only have salt for flavoring. Later, we also got hot water in the mornings so we could enjoy instant coffee. There were no 3-in-1 coffee packets made up of instant coffee, creamer, and sugar in those days—instant noodles and plastic bags had just recently arrived in Myanmar and I first saw them while in jail.

By 9 a.m. it would be bathtime. In the cold season nobody wanted to bathe first except me because I enjoyed cold baths—so I was, rain or shine, the first to bathe. After that I would smear thanakha paste over my face, put on my red lipstick, and be ready for the day. Sitting under the window, leaning against the wall, I would make tatted lace, crochet, or knit, chatting with my friends in other cells.

Lunch came about 10 a.m. The steaming rice in large square wooden bins was carried on a yoke by two male prisoners who were on kitchen duty. Another pair would bring in the soup, chickpea in the mornings and vegetable in the evenings. At our red door, women prisoners on rice duty would take over and bring them in. Men and women convicts couldn't speak with each other, but sometimes, husband and wife would be in jail at the same time and the guards allowed them to exchange a few words if both were assigned to this rice duty.

In addition to the chickpea soup, we were given fried shrimp paste, of such poor quality that it was like eating black tar. Prisoners would line up to get their plates and bowl, and then the food. The poorer prisoners ate heaped plates of rice soaked in soup. They could get as much rice as they wanted, but no seconds, and they usually managed to polish off a huge plateful. We all shared the food we received from home and with our rations, this made adequate meals. We ate in our cells, separated by walls, but we all ate at the same time so we could have a semblance of a communal, family meal.

In the afternoon we would be allowed out for exercise in turn, which meant walking in the yard or if it were raining, up and down our corridor. After that we usually napped or knitted, and at around 3 p.m. we in the cells would have another bath. After that we'd have tea from the hot water brought to us around that time, with instant coffee or green tea leaves, and some cookies. Every time we ate something we would share it with our friends, sending the food through the guards.

The evening rice came around 4 p.m. along with the special hospital diet. The soup for every inmate's evening meal was always made with vegetables, spinach, watercress, or mustard greens boiled together with a little salt. It was never tasty—sometimes it was even gritty with sand, but when it was made from the "wild" spinach that had stems an inch thick, it was great—the stems dissolved in your mouth. I could never find it in the outside world; it was grown in the gardens outside of the walls. They also grew kailan, mustard greens, pumpkins, or sweet potatoes (for the leaves) in any available space around the cells or halls.

The nutritional supplement consisted of a hard-boiled egg each, clear chicken broth, and a piece of chicken. When there wasn't enough to go around, the younger political prisoners in the halls weren't given any, or they would have to share or take turns. Preference was given to the older inmates.

Then everyone was locked up again at 5 p.m. and another head count taken. After that we chatted, and perhaps someone would sing, or tell stories. In the halls they prayed together at about 8:30 p.m. Taps was played from the upper story of the main gate at 9 p.m. Talking after taps was officially not allowed, but was ignored as long as we whispered.

It was a time when we longed for books. I missed the piles of beloved books I had at home, many of them read over and over but still with pleasure.

Due to the negotiations between the government and the International Committee of the Red Cross, prisoners by late 2003 or early 2004 were allowed to have books and a television set for weekends (if they chipped in to buy one), which meant greater privileges than we in our time ever saw. They could even write to and receive letters from family and friends. (I feel great admiration and gratitude for the ICRC's work, which helps many political prisoners.) A few years later, famous monks began to give Buddhist Vipassana meditation lessons in the prisons of Mandalay and Yangon, which were highly successful.

Prisoners weren't allowed to have any sharp instruments or things that could be sharpened and used as shivs; this meant that toothbrush handles were sometimes cut off at the men's section, so they couldn't be sharpened to a dangerous point. (We women were allowed toothbrushes with normal handles because Myanmar women are seldom violent, either in or out of jail. On the women's side there were few violent confrontations between prisoners.) The precaution regarding weapons was essential to keeping peace within the ranks of the male prisoners, for quarrels could lead to violence.

When the prison was overpopulated many inmates were moved out to the rock-breaking camps in the countryside. Criminals liked to go there because although the work was hard, they could be outdoors and earn a few *kyat* as pocket money. Because these places were easy to escape from, no political prisoners were sent there but the criminals were eager to try their luck.

When immediate family members of the opposite sex were in jail at the same place and time, they were allowed to meet once a month, in what we called Inner Visits. Since men and women had family visits on different days, imprisoned husbands and wives couldn't see their relatives together at the same time. Conjugal visits weren't allowed, but there were strong rumors that one famous Communist leader jailed in the 1970s bribed prison officials so he could have two of his numerous wives visit him privately on separate occasions, with each wife unaware of the other, of course.

For criminal women convicts, punishment for the poorest or most unruly was to carry out and clean the night soil jars, or to receive beatings on the calves with a bamboo or cane rod. Once a vagrant woman bit the cheek of a young mother until it bled, and she got a thorough lashing. Everyone thought she deserved it, for she had been tyrannizing women smaller than she for some time, taking away their food.

If women political prisoners broke the rules, their punishment was usually to have no visitors for a month, or in serious cases to be kept in isolation in one of the cells. Then their windows were closed for added discomfort, they weren't allowed to bathe or have family visits, nor could they receive food from the outside.

The isolation cells in the men's side were different, I heard, somewhat airless with only a small window high up on the wall. The electric light was kept on at all times as it was on the women's side, so prison employees could see what was going on.

Our cells, before they were renovated some six months before I was released, were separated by two layers of wooden planks set close together to prevent the inmates from passing things to each other. Actually mice had gnawed holes in the planks, so it was rather easy to see our neighbors as we talked together or passed each other small bits of food wrapped in plastic.

Those of us kept in the cells were allowed fifteen minutes outside other than the time we were given to bathe. But isolation wasn't as forlorn as it could have been with a busy office next door, where incoming prisoners and the ones being released had their information processed. This was where inmates coming back from visits had their food bags checked and all bits of paper removed.

Political prisoners during my time weren't beaten for nonpolitical offenses, ever since the time one of them was once beaten by accident. She was caught in a crowd of battling criminals when a jailer had waded in with a bamboo stick. She raised a fuss that resulted in a strict rule against any physical mistreatment of political prisoners, although at the time the term *political prisoner* was never used either in jail or in the media. In jail political prisoners were all called *Ngar Nya* or Section 5 (E). (Since *nya* also means "night" and *ngar* means "five," the *Ngar Nya* often joked that their sentence indicated they should be in jail for only five nights, so why were they here for years?)

If Section 5 (E) prisoners weren't bent on creating political unrest, the jailers pretty much left us alone; I was 10 (A) but because I had been involved in politics I was also called a 5 (E) at times. Most of us were educated and not of the lower classes so the guards accorded us the same respect they would give to us in the outside world.

They weren't the sadistic type of people you see in movies; they too were Myanmar people, innately friendly and caring. They were mostly good sorts, some less so and some better. In time, you made friends with some of the guards. Those who were strict feared we would break rules and they would get into trouble for it.

(In mid-May of 1990, all prisoners who had not yet been sentenced were allowed to prevote for the elections to be held on the twenty-seventh. We were given pens and slips of paper with the names of the candidates for the townships where we lived. Someone I knew and liked, U Khin Maung Swe of the NLD, was the candidate for Sanchaung Township and I wrote down his name in the space provided.

I was the only eligible voter living in the sentenced inmates' compound, but in the other women's section there were nearly two hundred who were still facing charges. The next day the guards wearily told me that instead of writing the name of the candidate as they should, they all insisted on writing the name Daw Aung San Suu Kyi on the ballot. They knew her name and wanted no one else, nor did they know, or care, that the NLD was her party. The guards had tried to explain that writing her name would invalidate the ballots, but no one listened. "All these votes down the drain," the guards told me in frustration.)

When the jailers got to know us well, after a year or so, the cell doors were usually left unlocked from morning to evening. Even then we didn't mingle all day long; we usually remained in the privacy of our cells unless we went to have coffee together out in the yard in the mornings or walked together among the vegetable patches in the evenings— while stealing baby string beans or okra, which are delicious when eaten raw.

In the evenings after the 5 p.m. lockup, we in our cellblock would tell stories or sing. Some of us could sing really well, but not me.

On special days, there would be a festival or theatrical concert going on beyond the walls, and we could hear faint music. Then everyone would fall silent, listening to the festivities.

By 9 p.m. I would fall back on my pallet, thankful that there was one less day to endure. The nights before sleep were rather difficult with memories of friends and family rushing around in my head.

If I didn't fall asleep quickly, I would idly swat at mosquitoes humming around my head. The mosquito bites in prison didn't seem to be as itchy as they felt outside, a phenomenon I cannot explain; maybe my "denial survival mode" was working well. They also flew more slowly in prison, or maybe I had more time; I could catch as many as twenty in a night. The tiny grey stiffening corpses would lie in a small pile by my "pillow" of a sweater, giving me great satisfaction.

I welcomed sleep. On lucky nights my dreams were filled with home, family, friends, and thrilling escapes or releases, but I knew that as soon as I opened my eyes in the morning and saw the same walls, my spirits could again plummet into a black pit of despair. As if physically pulling something heavy out of a deep well, I needed all my concentration to lift up my spirits and not let go, so they wouldn't go crashing back down into darkness.

5. SETTLING IN

When I first arrived in prison, on my first night I thought I would die if I were still there in a week. After a week had passed, I thought I would surely go mad in a month. After six months of imprisonment, and having experienced several heart-stopping rumors of amnesty, I decided that this constant dashing of hopes was too much for my mental health. Being under Section 10 (A) meant that I could be detained for up to three years without being charged: or, according to a new law later passed in 1990, five years.

I couldn't be on tenterhooks like this; it was too mentally exhausting. I told myself that I'd be damned if I would care anymore. If I were to be set free, I would find that out when the time came. I then settled down to a more comfortable state of mind, deciding to put my thoughts in order and to enjoy myself as much as I could.

Before I received a crochet hook, knitting needle, or tatting bobbin, I was almost a nervous wreck. Early on I had given Khet the phone number of friends, and asked that when she was released to tell them I was well and ask them to please send in my tatting bobbin and reels of cotton. As she went without being sentenced for two weeks, we both thought she would surely go free but we were mistaken.

After she was sentenced and had a chance to meet with her family, she asked them to relay my message to my friends. It was such a kindness, that in a short and emotional first visit with her family she thought of my needs and used up precious minutes on my behalf. When my first parcel came the following Monday, there were my bobbin and thread tucked into a loaf of bread.

That kept me sane, to be able to sit with busy hands while my mind roamed all over the world. While my fingers flew, my mind flew over the past, very carefully selecting memories that gave me pleasure, or weaving daydreams of such splendid unreality that they surpassed any fantasy movie. Mere illusions, but when reality is harsh, illusions are necessary.

Books or papers were no longer allowed after some male prisoners had written slogans on torn pages and sent them outside. I longed for a dictionary so I could improve my vocabulary or teach others. I desperately yearned to paint and worried that my hand might lose its touch if it had to go for years without holding a brush. I often painted in my imagination, choosing colors and making brushstrokes, and when I began painting after my release, I found out my hand had not been weakened through disuse.

I missed my books, and my music collection which ranged from the classics to Al Stewart to Grover Washington Jr. I missed seeing colors and hungered so much for something pretty that when someone gave me a packet of colorful jujube candies, I wiped away the sugar grains with a damp cloth and wrapped each small jelly cube tightly in clear plastic. I tied them together into a block and tucked it into the screen of my window where the light shone through it, making it look like a miniature piece of stained glass. This work of art lasted for over a year, all the time that I was in that cell.

In almost all of my waking hours I made lace and daydreamed or wrote novels in my head. Actually I wrote three which I thought weren't bad; I repeated each line in my head over and over so I wouldn't forget a word.

Later, after I got out, I began to paint furiously and when I finally began to write in earnest, I only wrote nonfiction. Of the three novels I had committed to memory, I had forgotten only one. The other two remained almost as fresh as when they were new but I had lost all interest in writing fiction. Perhaps after living with my daydreams for such a long time, I came to prefer reality.

From the top of the three steps at the back of my cellblock I could see the upper part of a leafless tree beyond the wall to the west; I saw it against so many moods of the sky and sunsets. The tree had dry branches that fanned out like a beautiful sculpture. We all admired it; scenery we could actually see, outside of our imaginations, was a rare thing.

When *kailan* was planted along the northern wall of our block, we were amazed at how beautiful and delicate the white flowers were.

We could see birds, and every evening it lifted our hearts to see them flying home, some in formation, and others singly or in chattering groups. I especially loved the white paddy birds, their feathers glazed a golden red in the evening sunlight.

In the early monsoon season, a few clumps of grass would grow in the cracks on top of the wall. When hit by the slanting morning or evening sunlight the tender grass tips became translucent and tipped with gold. I would stare at them for minutes on end. They seemed to symbolize a fragile but defiant presence on the blackened walls.

During the day and in the evening we watched cloud formations and at night, when my cell was on the sunny face of our block, I could see the stars.

The string bean garden at the back was the most wonderful place I saw in prison. Bamboo runners had been set up closely and thick vines were soon twined all over them. The flowers were lovely, in deep pinks and mauves and blues and soon butterflies were thick all over them. To walk there was like being in a fairy tale; we could see the black walls just beyond this enchanted garden but when butterflies fluttered around our heads, the walls lost their power to cause despair.

* * *

The first thing I noticed after I had settled down and refused to be on the constant lookout for freedom was that most of everyone's thoughts were on food—the lack of, dreams of, habit of, smuggling of, choice of, preparation of, creation of, obtaining of, stealing of, talking of. We begged it from friends; we shared it with friends. Food took up a lot of our time.

There were a few things that we had to rely on the guards to get, such as a relish made from boiled pickled fish, pounded chilies, and garlic called *nga pi yay*. For some reason, during most of the time I was in prison, this wasn't allowed in our food parcels. The fish-paste relish given out at mealtimes was adequate for a lot of the poorest vagrants, who said that at least they didn't have to worry about getting two solid meals a day. But all of us women loved nga pi yay, which wasn't easy to come by because it had to be made fresh from boiled fish that were almost putrid. Poor women who didn't have families visiting them usually had to wheedle it out of the nicer guards.

The food we lacked, and desired, and obtained from a kind guard if we were extremely lucky, was *monhinga*, rice noodles in a fish and lemongrass broth, our country's national dish. If we had this we shared, even if we each only ate a spoonful.

Hein, a wealthy businesswoman, was sentenced for smuggling gems and had her family bring monhinga at every visit. She would never share it, although she generously gave away other food such as apples or chocolates.

We missed ice, especially in the summer. One hot night a guard brought us a lump of it that she had taken from her husband's drinking party. That was the only time I tasted ice during my three years in jail.

How we longed for ice cream or faluda, the Indian dessert made with pink rose syrup, bits of jelly, thick milk, a lump of pudding, and a scoop of ice cream, served in large beer mugs, but we had to wait until we had our freedom to enjoy these treats.

Creation and preparation of food took a lot of ingenuity, as we had no fire. We made stuff like salads from raw papaya leaves (very bitter, tried once but never again), purloined young string beans stolen from the yard and eaten raw (utterly delicious), bunches of mustard greens (not bad when dipped in hot water). I would gather the ripened fruits of roselle, cut away the thick red petals covering the hard pods, and steep them in hot water. The water turned a nice red with a sour taste and, when mixed with sugar, made a refreshing kind of lemonade.

Roselle pods, raw salad leaves, and the precious string beans had to be stolen from the garden beds around our block. They were meant to be sent to the kitchens—but not if we got to them first. As the food parcels came once a week (and in the first months of our incarcerations these parcels weren't allowed to contain fresh vegetables in case we got tummy upsets), we longed for greens.

Stealing these when a jailer's back was turned for a minute was fun. When cranky Mother Kyi scolded us for it, I would say to her before I picked any, "Hey, old mother, I'm going to steal some mustard greens, turn your back!" She would be so flummoxed at my making her an accessory to my crime that she could only stare away from me, furiously puffing on her large cheroot as I plucked what I wanted. Later she and other guards would turn their backs and stare off into space if they suspected us of stealing the greens.

I never saw a pumpkin (maybe earlier birds than I got them) but their golden-colored flowers were lovely, and delicious in soup. Toss whole flowers in a good clear stock and it made the prettiest soup in the world. There were also sweet potato plants thriving in long rows just under the windows of our cellblock. We call sweet potatoes *kazun u*, or egg of the *kazun* plant. *Kazun* is water spinach or morning glory, and its leaves are used in soups or stir-fried with garlic. A poor man's dish, it is nevertheless a favorite vegetable of the Myanmar people. The leaves of both kazun and kazun u are similar in taste but the sweet potato leaves have a tougher texture.

We often fantasized about preparing the food we missed most, never mind that we probably didn't know how to cook these dishes in real life. In our block we could talk to each other if we weren't too loud, and in our imaginations we would cook duck or coconut rice or anything we fancied. Our cooking fantasies drove others mad, making them hungrier than ever, as they heard us reporting to each other on how we were stirring the soup or testing the meat for tenderness. I even made Peking duck that in reality would have been quite inedible.

Not long after our imaginative stint that drove others wild, some guards had small electric stoves going on their desks to warm up their lunch (hidden when the jailer was present). Through negotiations brokered by Pyone in return for her astrology predictions, they would cook us the delicious *chin yay* sour soups we loved so much. Into the pot would go the leaves of sweet potato, kailan, or mustard greens together with fried nga pi kyaw or dried prawns we always had in our "larders," our plastic bags hanging on the wall. The soup was seasoned with tamarind paste the guards brought for us. We never tasted anything so good.

We would have them heat up the chicken soup and chicken we received every evening, drop in some pumpkin flowers, and bring us some wonderful soups. We also pooled our daily ration of hard-boiled eggs to be cooked into a curry, using nga pi kyaw as a gravy base and seasoning it with the Indian spice powder the guards brought us from their homes. This made such a wonderful change from the steamed or deep-fried dishes that we were given almost daily.

Once I collected pennywort roots from other prisoners who had been sent bunches of these green plants. I dug a wide and shallow bed near the water tank near the front of our block and planted them, every week a few more. In a few months, there was a wide, thick bed of the fresh, bright green pennywort sprigs for everyone to enjoy. They had a minty taste with medicinal value, and made a good salad.

Near the red gate there was one very small and scraggly wild gooseberry bush. I proclaimed that the fruit was all mine, unnecessarily as it turned out, for no one else wanted to eat it. To save the berries from the birds I had to eat them before they were ripe but I still thought they were a great treat.

The first cold season I went through in prison at the end of 1989 was colder than usual; in fact it was frigid. Since food allowances were strict at the time, I couldn't get sugar or milk powder. I will never forget how for days I longed to have some to mix with my early morning gruel. When I finally got a few spoonfuls sent by my friend Tin, it tasted sublimely delicious.

Food parcels had to last two weeks for sentenced prisoners and for us detainees, one. Some sentenced prisoners formed groups who would stagger their visits so that their group would enjoy a parcel every week. They all ate together, sharing what they had.

The fresh-cooked dishes we loved were stir-fried vegetables, noodles, or watery fish curry with coriander, tomatoes, and green chilies. For me, a dish I often had that others loved as well was pickled sour bamboo shoots cooked with pork belly. That dish had a distinct aroma that made us all hungry. As it was quite sour enough already I could keep it for up to four days. Perhaps it often went bad but at the time I had a cast-iron stomach so it was all right. However, I was careful not to give any to others after the second day. The way we ate, it was a miracle we didn't come down with ptomaine.

The food we prepared without a cooking fire was most often based on the nga pi kyaw sent in by our families, the dried shrimp or fish pounded until it was fluffy and then fried with onions and chili. We mixed it with finely shredded leaves of whatever edible plant was on hand to make a salad. For knives, we used the tops of tin cans if we could find any. If we got hold of any rusty piece of metal we would polish it carefully on a stone to make knives for our cooking.

Nga pi kyaw in one form or other was the staple in all food parcels and you could get really tired of this dish after several months of it. Since it kept well, dried salted fish was also another staple. After our release one of us said that when she heard a vendor hawking dried salted fish in front of her house she felt like running out to clobber him, and I couldn't face nga pi kyaw for three years after I left Insein.

Thinking and talking about the food we would eat as soon as we were out took up a large portion of time but once I was out in the world, I didn't rush to eat the food that had been on my list. I had no appetite. The others told me it was the same with them. Craving for food apparently has power only in prison.

* * *

We begged our families or friends to send in those frivolous things that are utterly essential to life—dangly earrings, nail polish, and for me, red lipstick when I used up the five tubes I brought in with me.

The friend I asked unfortunately was a confirmed bachelor at the time, not yet having the luck to find the young, beautiful, and extremely intelligent wife he has now. When I asked him for red lipstick, he couldn't tell anyone for whom he was buying it, as I wasn't supposed to be in contact with anyone outside. But he had no idea where he could buy anything like this; his one sister was living in Mandalay, all his other siblings were male, and he couldn't ask his sisters-in-law just in case they reported to his mother that he was perhaps purchasing gifts for a secret girlfriend.

Finally he confided in a woman colleague at work, without mentioning who it was for. However, she thought he had finally, thank God, found a girlfriend and spread the news with a hallelujah. It reached the ears of every single one of his friends and acquaintances, and he had to confess to some of our mutual friends that hush, hush, it was for her, drat that woman, even from jail she managed to get him into trouble. (One of my artist friends, Khin One, said that at this point he stopped worrying about how I was faring: if I was wearing red lipstick in jail, I was sure to be fine.)

Finally after two months the lipstick arrived: not red but a beige-pink. In the uproar my bachelor benefactor had completely forgotten my color choice.

* * *

In the evenings we took turns telling stories, movies, or novels. I told *Gone with the Wind*, which took three days and was a major project because those who had seen the movie or read the novel's Burmese translation would remind me of things I forgot and left out. There were many arguments about which scenes came first, and did Rhett really say that?

Of Mice and Men I related first to a friend who took over from me to tell the whole cellblock, because I couldn't get through to the end without crying. At the end of that particular storytelling session everyone broke down and sobbed; for days afterward any mention of "rabbits" resulted in tears.

I also retold *The Unconquered*, a short story by Somerset Maugham in which a French girl drowned her baby who had been conceived when she was raped by a German soldier during World War II. He had been violent only on that occasion and he was delighted at the thought of being a father, dreaming of how he would bring up his son. He also became very good to the girl and her family, bringing them food; her parents began to like him, but she couldn't. At the end of this the girls shrieked in horror: "Aunty Lay! How could you tell us this horrible, horrible story?" and then sulked for half a day. After that when I suggested storytime, they would ask me suspiciously exactly what sort of story I was planning to tell.

Singing was a talent especially appreciated; it brought instant joy to the listener. One misty morning in December, Pyone and I, in separate cells but next to each other, heard a snatch of a song we both loved about meeting a lover in the "Mist of Winter." It was sung by a Thirty D walking past our window with a toilet basin in her hands, on her way to clean it. Pyone and I burst out laughing as the girl sashayed on her way.

There was one young woman in our block who had a lovely voice and knew a great many songs. She was a college graduate who was under a death sentence for beheading a woman during the crowd hysteria of 1988. We would put in our requests, and I noticed we all chose slow songs of love and heartbreak. Before half of the prisoners in our block, including our diva, were transferred to the one in the other women's section, her concerts would start at about seven in the evening up until taps. Even the guards missed her melodies when she left.

I was surprised to discover that I missed music more than I missed books. Once I suffered horrendously when someone who was very untalented played taps for three weeks; he was probably just learning. It was so horrible with off-key or missed notes that while he struggled I would chew dried crusts of bread. That crunching sound was the only thing loud enough to drown him out.

However, about three months before I left, a true musician took on this duty. He played so well that I sent a message of thank-you through a guard, and from that point it got even better with jazzy flourishes. It was sheer delight to lie in bed and listen to it and for once, during all the nights he played, I didn't sink into the despair which usually hit me around that time of night. I never knew his name and by now he is probably retired, but what a musician he was.

Tin Thein, a lifer for accessory to murder, was another fine singer. She could tell a good story, too, playing the different parts, like the traditional *Kwet Seit* storytellers who once roamed the countryside, with villagers crowding around them to listen to old tales. On late afternoons the jailer would call, "It's so boring, Tin Thein! Give us a *Kwet Seit* story!" Being the performer she was, if there was any part of the classical story she had forgotten, Tin Thein would make up something to fill the gap, incongruous or not, and carry on to the end. No one complained and I long ago had given up any attempt to keep her to the script.

One night, looking toward the upper story of the hall from my window, I could see people walking around with red and green plastic basins on their heads. I wondered what on earth they were up to but I should have known it was one of Tin Thein's projects.

The jailer noticed the going-ons when she heard loud outbursts of laughter and sent Ma Nwei the guard to check it out. I could see Ma Nwei mounting the stairs and when she reached the door, she suddenly bent over, convulsed with laughter. She then stood enjoying what she saw, still laughing, so the jailer sent another guard who also didn't come back. Finally the jailer had to go and see for herself.

Tin Thein was presenting a play with herself as playwright, director, and star. It was a well-known classic made famous by the great dancer Shwe Mann Tin Maung, based on the life of an eighteenth-century poet, Let-wei Thundara. Of course Tin Thein added her own fabricated touches, as could be expected.

I found out later those wearing basins on their heads were ministers who, in our old royal court, wore high velvet turbans of red or green. Attendants to the king and queen waved fans that were brooms. Bodyguards stood at attention pretending to hold swords. The king and queen had almost no speaking parts but wore thick makeup and were draped with dangly earrings, brooches, and other finery collected from the audience. Tin Thein at the high point of the play sang the famous classic song that the poet had sent to the king about his exile in the icy northern jungles, which made the monarch immediately take pity upon him and let him come home.

She also inserted a few improbable scenes, never before or after presented in any play or biography about this great poet. One was when Let-wei Thundara's wife gave birth while he was in exile. The birth scene, so I was told, was a great hit. Shorty, the most irrepressible and youngest of all political prisoners, played the baby, with a taller woman as the mother in childbirth.

"I did it quite realistically," the mother told us smugly the next day. "I'd seen so many real births in the clinic."

"I was a great baby," Shorty said, not willing to be outshone and delighted by her fame. "I was crying like this…waaa…aaah, waa…aaah…WAAAH!" she wailed, until we all told her to please shut up and go away.

We still relish the stories of the pranks we played on each other. One April Fool's Day I took my friend Nita's mirror that she hung on her window and then I waited in vain all day for her squeals of rage. She was so silent the whole day that I began to wonder if she hadn't yet noticed it was missing.

Finally at bedtime I casually mentioned to her that when I was outside, I had not seen her mirror on the window. She said it had been stolen and she didn't want to make a fuss, but she had been feeling miserable all day. I confessed and gave it back immediately with a guard but even today I still feel sorry for my joke that misfired.

* * *

Once Hein smuggled in about three yards of thin white muslin and then, realizing it wouldn't work as a mosquito net, gave it all to me. With a borrowed pair of small scissors, I cut and sewed two maternity jackets, edged with crocheted lace, for my pregnant friend Nita. At the time, she still lived in the hall and she told me later that when I sent the jackets over to her, Shorty and her pals grabbed them first. They stuffed towels under the jackets, played at being pregnant, and refused to give the clothing back to Nita for two days. Having attended all the births in the clinic, uninvited, in spite of Aunty Hpaw's protests, these girls already had firsthand knowledge of what went on during labor and were able to act out giving birth quite realistically.

Nita told me that they went around with bellies stuck out, moaning that their contractions were getting nearer or that their water broke "just now." Pyone was exasperated at unmarried young girls pretending to give birth, but her threats didn't stop the games. Pyone threatened a lot but what she gave out were snacks she prepared herself such as noodle salad or fruit cups with milk powder and sugar, and the girls knew that.

I also made cloth turtles from small scraps of fabric that a guard brought for me, as her sister was a seamstress and had a lot of small remnants left over after making a garment. I stuffed the turtles with cotton wool when I could get some or with the pieces of fabric I couldn't use. The turtles' backs were patchwork, the edges of the shells another design, with different colored legs, tail, and head. I gave them away to friends who would send them out to their children. I was allowed under supervision by a guard to cut the pieces with a tiny pair of scissors and I would cut a big batch at a time, only returning the scissors after I had trimmed my hair.

(Among the very conservative middle classes it wasn't done for women my age to have short hair. One woman convicted for gambling lived next door to a famous artist I knew, which I discovered just as she was being processed to be released. I asked her to give my regards to her neighbor and to tell him not to worry about me. She saw me with my short haircut and thought that my hair was growing out because I had been punished with head shaving. She did pass on my regards but also added that my head had been shaved, the news of which swept like wildfire among my artist friends. However, they soon figured out that somehow I was managing to cut my hair.)

In the halls, the girls learned to play chess, carving the pieces out of different colored soap with a bit of sharp bamboo. May May Than, another political prisoner, was particularly good at this; she could carve a whole chess set beautifully while holding a conversation. Someone else carved lovely figures of Kwan Yin and Buddha images from soap which we could buy with cheroots.

Even before I landed in jail, I had heard of prisoners making *Kyo Badee*, the Buddhist prayer beads, out of string, but had never seen these and couldn't imagine how a string (*Kyo*) could be made into beads (*Badee*). One woman who watered the plants under my window told me that she knew how to make them. She described the process in detail and I began to make the beads the next day.

It was easy enough: you needed something round with a hole through it as a base for each bead. I made this out of strands of wool soaked in my morning gruel and then wrapped around a smooth, thin rod of bamboo. When this was dry and hard, I had a strong base with a smooth bore.

Over it I embroidered tight loops starting at one end of the opening and toward the other so that the bead would be covered with a neat, wavelike pattern. Using a crochet hook I tucked the leftover length of string under the stitched surface. I didn't make prayer beads, however. I made necklaces, using different colored wool and varying the size of the beads, with pom-poms attached at the end of the strings, rather elegant, I must say. I gave many of these away to my friends and they would wear them for family visits. Other women crocheted shawls and scarves for me; we were constantly making things for each other.

From the time I was a child I knew how to knit or crochet simple patterns and now, with so much time on my hands, I learned more complicated designs. We weren't allowed to have proper metal knitting needles so I stole a bamboo stick that Ma Nwei the guard used to keep rowdy vagrants in line. Using a small piece of thin metal I cut it into two needles, smoothing the sides and tips carefully. Within an hour I was done, just in time to see Ma Nwei scratching her head and looking all over, asking, "Has anyone seen my stick?"

I called to her and waved my bamboo knitting needles at her, grinning. For a moment she looked baffled, but then, realization dawned that her stick was gone forever. She flapped her hands at me in resignation and went off to get another one.

I made a few knitted sweaters for my friends and me but they were all too short in the waist as I was always too impatient to get them done. I also crocheted scarves and shawls, which being lacy took less time to complete. Making tatted lace was too time-consuming even if I did have all the time in the world, but it was nice to have something that needed a lot of concentration during dire times of misery when even jokes or songs didn't work.

* * *

In prison, it is not unusual for strange dreams to come true.

Dreams in a jail cell were somehow more vivid; everything would be sharply, clearly etched. I knew I was dreaming, and I would carefully watch what was happening. After we awoke, we would try to work out what our dreams meant, and someone who was considered an expert would be consulted at times. In our block this was a woman named Mar Mar.

Two or three times I dreamed of getting a gift of diamonds, or choosing diamonds other than rubies when offered a choice. Mar Mar told me that rubies meant good luck and wealth, while diamonds meant a hard but honorable life. The color yellow or gold also meant honor, but it depended upon other things in the dream whether it meant honor with freedom or not. I joked that next time I should at least take or receive a small ruby but it never happened; I always chose or was given the diamonds that somehow represented hardship.

On several occasions when it looked as if I was to be released with many other detainees, my dreams vividly told me I would be staying on…and I did.

Once, in December 1989, a whole bunch of us were being interrogated. At the time even these intelligence officers were sure of our release and looked happy about it, for our sessions were keeping them extremely busy with not enough sleep. Unfortunately the higher authorities obviously decided otherwise, for the night after my interrogation I had a dream that dashed all hopes.

The wife of my ex-husband had just given birth to their first child, their only son. When I had this dream I had not heard about the birth or the sex of the baby although I knew the approximate due date.

I dreamed that I had been released, and friends came to visit me in a house where I used to live in my childhood. My mother was sitting next to me on the highly polished wooden floor in the large drawing room with three French windows on each side. Many friends were sitting around us and Tin, who according to the dream had been released for some time, was also there. A boy of perhaps three was running around and then came to sit on my knee. It was the son of my ex-husband, whom I knew—even in my dream—was really just a few days old. As soon as I woke up, I realized that I wouldn't get out until the boy was about that age, and it was true. The child was about three when I finally met him and he looked very much as he had in my dream.

Another time there were yet again strong rumors of a general amnesty and in my dream I was preparing to leave, combing my hair, which came down to my waist. I had been trimming my hair with a nail clipper so it would never grow that long. I knew when I woke up that my hair, if I left it uncut, would be that long only after three years' time.

Then a few months later, rumors again swept our cellblock about an amnesty, prompting a dream that I was free and planning to buy a flat. When I went to see it, I found the walls had been painted black and there were no windows. I woke up miserable, knowing there would be no release for me. It was true: a couple of days later Ma Ma Myint was free and I wasn't. That was in May of 1990.

In December of that year, I dreamed I saw a stranger's face in a cell window, a slender, pale lady with a thin, oval face, wearing a pink-beige homespun jacket. The next evening a group of prisoners was brought in to prison and one of them was the person of my dream, although I had never seen her before in real life. Her face was exactly the one that I saw in my dream and she wore the same pink-beige jacket.

I often had dreams of going home but, strange to say, every dream ended with me voluntarily returning to prison. I would hit myself on the head when I woke up, that I could be so stupid as to come back. In my dreams I would stand in line to come through the gate with many others apparently on the same mission. I would hide something under my clothes that I had been longing to have in reality, such as a thick novel or a bottle of pink nail polish. Once I had Lawrence Durrell's *Alexandria Quartet* under my panties, sticking out like a brick on my belly; I still wonder how I imagined, even in a dream, that I could hide that big a bump.

* * *

Something strange happened in our block the night before three girls were suddenly released after four months. By then almost all hope for them was gone, for if you are not out within a month, it usually meant you would stay at least three years.

We all believe geckoes cry often when foretelling good news and that night, the geckoes in our block had been unbelievably noisy, chirping until daybreak. Most of us commented on it the next morning, and by late afternoon the girls were out.

The same thing happened the night before Ma Ma Myint was released.

The strangest and scariest event had to be the Great Haunting. It happened one night in the upper story of the hall in the next compound where Pyone and Tin lived.

That day, as evening fell, I kept getting goose bumps that came and went. At about 9 p.m., just after taps, some of us in our cellblock were settling down to sleep, praying, meditating, or telling beads. The women in the hall were either lying in bed or sitting up to chat in whispers. It was a relaxed, peaceful time but too early for anyone to fall asleep. All of a sudden I heard an eerie wail of many voices rising to a crescendo as if in one voice. We all heard it: many voices rising in unison, a cry full of chilling despair.

I thought, as others in our block did, that it was the prisoners in the hall who were crying out in terror at something. But no, it wasn't the prisoners upstairs or downstairs. They also heard it, first coming from outside and through the barred doors and then engulfing them, sweeping over and around them. Immediately after that wail I heard loud scattered screams and sounds of pounding feet. That was the inmates running around in panic.

From what I found out from Pyone and Tin later (two of the most practical, intelligent, and observant people I know and the least likely to imagine something like this), first they all heard a soft wail, and looked around to see who it was. Suddenly the wail intensified into a loud sound unlike anything made by a human, and some prisoners started screaming in terror.

The less excitable, Tin and Pyone among them, saw that in a space where the poorest vagrants sleep near the far end of the hall, a group of women stood in a circle as they fought, scratching at each other. Their hair swung long and loose, covering their faces so no one could see who they were. They had on the white prison uniform, Tin said, but she noticed their clothing was very white, unlike the usual grimy near-brown ones worn by the vagrant girls. Those sitting nearby scrambled away in fear. The electric lights, usually a yellowish glow, shone white at that time and fell on the fighting group like a soft spotlight.

Younger girls around Tin were clutching at her in fear, so she turned to hush them. When she looked up again, the fighting group had vanished. Prisoners were running around like mad and there was total confusion. At first, none of them had any idea what had happened; they thought it had been a real fight but unlike at other times, all of them were terror-stricken. Later, some in our block said that at the sound of the wail, they had felt such a deep despairing misery that they couldn't control the sobs that rose in them. They said tears streamed down their faces. I was standing at my window and staring open-mouthed at the hall; while the wail didn't make me cry, I felt heart-thumping terror.

The prison authorities couldn't dismiss the idea that it was a plot to create unrest, rather than a supernatural occurrence, so for several days there were interrogations about the affair. On the whole, our stories tallied. I have no idea how it was written up in the report, but I heard from our guards that the jailers privately believed it was caused by ghosts, since they had experienced a few similar haunted episodes in the past.

One night, a group of Thirty D sitting near the door to their hall insisted they saw men in hats walking single file up the stairs and vanishing as they reached the top. The group described exactly the type of hats once worn by overseers in prison about fifty years ago, which was confirmed by the guards who had heard about this headwear from their fathers or uncles. Later I read about these hats in the biography of a jailer who served long before our time.

Another omen that we clung to—since even in normal life we are a superstitious people—was a belief in the significance carried by muscular twitches of certain parts of the body. The twitching of upper eyelids meant good luck and lower ones, bad. When the upper lip twitched, it meant you would get good food, the lower lip meant you would talk to people from far off places. A small muscle twitching in the upper right arm meant success or victory over adversaries. If this occurred in the upper left arm, it was still good fortune but on a lesser scale. Thighs or any part of the lower limbs twitching meant you walked—freedom!

Our most essential diversion was daydreaming, that indulgence in illusions that the Lord Buddha said is one of the three main things to avoid, along with greed and anger. Bad for our souls or not, illusions were very useful in jail. We imagined that good things were in store for us, that freedom was just around the corner, and that we were beautiful, talented, and successful in our fantasies that took us beyond our black walls.

Another thing that kept me sane was my curiosity. I have always been deeply interested in how the human psyche works ever since I was eleven years old and trying to make sense of the relationship between my beautiful, high-maintenance mother and my gentle, clever father. They were mad about each other and—maybe because of this—were constantly at each other's throats.

As a youngster I couldn't imagine the reasons behind the passion and anger they shared, until I realized these emotions need no reason. It took me a long time to discover the childhood baggage each carried and to understand what made them tick or, in Mum's case, explode. Now, with all this jailbird leisure time on my hands, I thought I would use it to my advantage to examine myself as well as the layers and nuances of the varieties of human nature around me.

6. FRIENDS

The best and most lasting lesson I learned from prison is that nothing in life is more important than steady, strong, and warm friendships.

If that weren't true, how could prisoners ever manage to be happy? We were in a place where living conditions were primitive, where the food wasn't at all what we were used to, and where we were unable to see our children grow up. True, I left neither offspring nor family behind—apart from my mother, who was a strong woman who didn't depend on me— but my friends in prison with families didn't huddle in corners weeping in despair.

Maybe they wept at night and maybe our happiness was a mask, but we laughed a lot. We used to say to each other that we wished
a) our families could see us like this so that they wouldn't worry any-more;
b) they couldn't see us like this, because if they knew we were having so much fun they would never send us food parcels again.

Perhaps we were in denial of the harshness of our imprisoned state, but whatever worked was fine with us.

(Years after my release I met a western freelance journalist who righ-teously said we must have been in denial if we thought we had good times and that we should have had the "courage and honesty" to face facts. I told her that if she, right now, went out to the street and distributed pamphlets against our government, she too would have a chance to see how she would face facts. It would be only a few days of fact facing, I assured her, since foreigners who did that sort of thing were usually put on the next flight out after a day or two of interrogation. She fled from my flat and I never saw her again.)

In order to conquer adversity and despair with calmness, we prisoners constantly did our best to keep each other's spirits up with songs, jokes, and stories of our lives. We Myanmar people tend not to dwell on tragedy but face life, however hard it may be, with humor. Nothing but the warmth and jokes of our friends could help us to bear the high black walls that held us in a confined space, this small space that was run like a world separate and different from all others that we had known; a world whose inmates, both rulers and the ruled, weren't companions that we would have chosen.

From the time I was thirty I practiced conscious awareness after reading a book on Zen Buddhism written by Dr. Thynn Thynn, who at present runs a meditation center in Los Angeles. Now I had the opportunity to delve deeper into my mind and to observe how other people in this very small world reacted to the situation they were in, and to each other.

In my early days in the block, my cell was Number 4, one cell away from the rear entrance, while the attorney Daw Myint Myint Khin (Ma Ma Myint) was in Number 1, a cell next to the front door. She was blunt of speech, a no-nonsense woman with a great, dry sense of humor, whose friendship and integrity I value to this day.

Myanmar people joke that straight-talking folk have to live outside the village because no one is able to stand their bluntness, which is often more like tactlessness. In our culture, to be forthright in speech is considered highly impolite.

She and I agreed that we live "outside the village," and we were both glad of it. Better to live outside of society, we decided, than to live under wimpy standards that prevent telling the truth for fear of offending others.

Every Tuesday the male senior jailers made their rounds to ask each prisoner what she needed or what her grievances might be. Ma Myint was always the first one they talked to because our cellblock was the first they saw when they entered our gate. In her calm and objective attorney's tone, without a hint of irony or sarcasm (a tone she used at all times, even when addressing her husband), she would list the things she needed. We quickly began calling her Gandawin Ayit, or "Classic Cranky," for her improbable requests, a name that stuck forever afterward.

"I am not being cranky," she explained calmly when we teased her. "I wasn't being sarcastic. I do really need an armchair; I'm too old to sit on the floor. My knees cannot take it and my back hurts. I could also do with a bed and perhaps a bedside table with some books."

Ma Ma Myint kept insisting that her requests were made in all innocence, but every week, the poor men would be forced to explain once again that her needs couldn't be met. Prisoners simply cannot sit in armchairs. Nor could they have a shelf of novels by their beds—or even have beds with mattresses. These senior jailers were always very polite to her but I imagined they really hated to stand at her window. Sometimes they would get so mad that they would forget to stop at our windows and would stomp off after their exchange with her. I told her that probably they did rock-paper-scissors each week to see who would ask her the question: "Is there anything you need?" There must have been jubilation and celebration in the Main Jail when she was released after nine months.

Although we gave each other a lot of support, it was impossible for everyone we met in prison to be our pals. Personalities differed and some rubbed grittily against others in a place of scant physical or mental elbow room. The only thing we could control was our reaction to other people's attitudes.

Both prisoners and guards could be warm and caring or selfish and demanding or a combination of both. People are born with their weaknesses and strengths and they can no more be blamed for certain characteristics than for having a crooked nose. In stressful situations, all basic instincts rise to the surface and in prison there is no hiding behind any social facades, as none exist. We learned a lot about human nature in prison and for me, who was there for barely three years, this was more of an educational experience than a tragic one.

In another cell in our block was a woman who had been arrested for foreign exchange infringements and was under the same detention as we were. We called her Mar Mar, and she would regale us with stories of her family: a husband who apparently existed happily under her thumb, a handsome grown-up son, and two pretty teenage daughters. She was horrified that any woman, me for example, should be divorced and, even worse, should actually enjoy being single, so she was determined to change my mind with her stories of happy family life.

Almost every night, she would talk to us, beginning a story innocently enough but ending with a moral message on the joys of marriage. I would see this coming before the end and would call out a local idiom, "Your train is going to pull into the same old station," at which point she would laugh and give up.

One of Mar Mar's favorite stories was how she had arranged, with great difficulty, a marriage for her son with the daughter of a very good family ("Stinking rich," she said, "plus beautiful and without a single slur upon her name"). Her son had been quite agreeable to the arrangement and the young couple was engaged with much fanfare. A month before the wedding, which was being planned with great and lavish detail, he met someone else at a friend's wedding where he was the best man and she the bridesmaid, and they promptly fell in love. He declared he would have no other.

"I practically had to grovel on my knees to the family of his fiancée," she wailed. "My husband and I wanted to cut off our faces in shame. We dared not accept any social invitations for months just in case we ran into them. Praise be to Allah"—Mar Mar was Muslim—"the girl married a very wealthy man soon afterward. My son eloped as soon as his engagement was broken, and his father and I actually urged him to. It would have been such bad form to hold a wedding for him after his disgraceful behavior. At least they both are really crazy about each other."

She would sigh deeply several times at the perfidy of the young and then chuckle with satisfaction that her son had found the love of his life. Unlike other mothers, she wasn't at all jealous of her daughter-in-law.

Ma Ma Myint, who is a notary as well as an attorney, went in cahoots with Mar Mar and cajoled me to promise that if she found me a bridegroom, I would marry in her presence and wouldn't have to pay her customary wedding fee.

"How much is it, anyway?" I demanded.

"Five hundred kyat." (About US$10 at the time)

"Five hundred kyat? And just to save that measly sum, I'm supposed to get married? Forget it," I declared.

"Not if you marry someone who brings a basket of gold and dies the same day. You stand to gain big-time," she offered.

"That I could handle," I said.

"But we go fifty-fifty with the loot," I generously promised. "You get half the basket. Just make sure he drops dead the same day, and of natural causes, please." So to this day this remains a standing promise.

These two supporters of matrimonial bliss were released in May of 1990 and I was left alone in the cellblock. On the day before she left, Ma Ma Myint came to my window to say goodbye. She looked miserable to leave me and asked what she should tell my mother. I told her to tell Mother not to try to get me out by asking favors of her college friends who had high connections, or else I would never speak to her again. Life in prison wasn't unbearable, at least not for someone who was a ragamuffin child and a bohemian adult. It would be the height of disgrace for me to get a special favor from high connections and abandon my friends.

(Ma Ma Myint still declines to accept any payment for the various contracts she has drawn up for me as she has so far failed to find me a rich-and-near-death husband. She remains as cranky and as sharply witty as ever. When I needed to sell off a small plot of land I had bought in 1986 I didn't even bother to read the contract she had drawn up for me before signing it. When I bought a flat with the proceeds, I still didn't read the contract. Both the buyers and the sellers thought I was a very nice person because I left all the tough talking to her.)

After I was alone in my cellblock for a few months, Pyone, my engineer friend, and a few other girls asked to be allowed to stay in the cells instead of living in the crowded hall. They remained with me until new arrivals needed the cells and I was very happy to have their company, even though I didn't mind being alone.

Pyone was a good astrologer; she would draw the necessary diagrams and numbers in the dust as we had no paper or pen, and predict the future, for free. She was the type who would never lie even if it killed her, and people trusted her. Every day she was busy with prisoners who were worried about families or business they had left outside. Even the jailers and guards consulted her from time to time.

(After our release Pyone helped me find the flat I now live in as she was working for the construction company that built it. She would tuck her longyi in carefully and climb bamboo scaffolding up five stories to see how the work was going. Her appearance revealed the person she was; her piercing eyes looked out from behind thick glasses, a well-shaped but thin mouth marked her decisive personality, and her square jaw showed her determination. Even after she fell ill in 1998 and lay bedridden and unable to speak for months before her death in 2003, the level, piercing look in her eyes remained unchanged.)

While she stayed in the cells, from her own supply of instant noodles she would prepare the spicy-sour noodle and rice salad we liked so much; she made this daily for our afternoon snack and sent a serving to everyone in our block. To it we added the tender kailan leaves that grew under our windows, softening them in hot water before we ate them.

It was from Pyone that I heard about the large patch of lemongrass growing near the halls, where she had liked to take walks while breathing in the fragrant air.

"That's the one thing I miss in the block," she would tell us. "But otherwise I like it here, I cannot stand the damn chatter; women talk too much."

She said that there were also a few beds of okra and that the tender fingerlings could be stolen and eaten raw as soon as they appeared. We learned to enjoy them and after we were released, we still ate okra raw, even when it was full-grown.

Near our cellblock we unfortunately didn't have lemongrass, but we did have the pennywort I planted and kailan, pumpkin, mustard greens, and string beans. There was one scraggly tomato plant that gave a lot of small fruit until rats gnawed its roots and one day it toppled over, dead.

Nita was another friend I had known outside but who became closer within our "inside family" circle. She was less than two months pregnant when she was arrested in November 1990. At the time she didn't even know she was pregnant; the younger of her two sons was by then in his teens.

We all hoped she would have a daughter who looked just like her; we all insisted on that because Nita was very pretty with dimpled cheeks, laughing eyes, and silky-smooth, creamy skin. Her hair was curly, and her smile captivated men even after she became a grandmother. Her husband, who passed away soon after she was released, was the sweetest man I have ever met, although not good-looking.

Nita and Pyone formed a duo, sharing their food and eating together before Nita was transferred to my cellblock. Pyone was ready to calculate the baby's astrological chart the minute it was born, but first she needed to know the precise time of birth.

Nita began labor pains one night and she was close to giving birth by three the next morning. A vehicle was called for to take her to Insein Hospital; it was the truck used to transport vegetables and Nita, already writhing in pain, had a very bumpy ride. Guard Ma Aye Mon went along too, and we repeatedly told her to please note the exact time of birth so Pyone could work out all astrological calculations.

None of us could go back to sleep, and we sat up waiting, worrying and hoping for a girl. When Ma Aye Mon returned, she called out triumphantly before she even came through the door: "Born at 6:22:12 a.m. exactly!"

We all applauded and then eagerly asked, as there were heavy bets going, "Was it a boy or girl?" She stood there stunned, her mouth hanging open, utterly stumped; she had forgotten to note that particular piece of information.

We were furious. After all, it could only be one or the other, we told her, and that was the first question anyone would ask at a birth. How difficult could that be? Ma Aye Mon had an excellent memory but under the pressure of getting the exact time she had blundered. She was mortified and sent a friend to go check at the hospital for us—it was a boy.

Nita's baby boy Akar stayed with her for a week in the hospital and then her husband took him home. It was six months before she saw her baby again.

Both she and the baby live in London now. Nita left the country with her children two years after her release. Akar grew up strong, handsome, highly intelligent, unafraid of anything, a young man who takes very good care of his mother.

In the cell next to mine were two women, Daw Yee and her daughter Snow, who was about twenty-eight years old. Snow's late father had been a midlevel Burma Communist Party member, but neither she nor her mother had ever been directly involved in politics until they met Ko Thet Khaing.

He was an important underground BCP member who needed a false identity to live above ground. Although already married to the daughter of a politburo member, in Yangon he pretended to be a husband to Snow and father to her two young daughters from her previous marriage. Her new "marriage" was strictly in name only because BCP members are extremely careful about their personal reputations.

This way Ko Thet Khaing was able to move freely. However, within a year he was captured with his "wife" and "mother-in-law." I think the military intelligence must keep a pretty close eye on those suspected of BCP connections and surely they had photos of all the important members. There probably were infiltrators on both sides.

Snow was a beautiful young woman, and as fair-skinned as her name. Her mother too must have been a beauty when she was young, we could see it. Now a plump, kindly woman in her sixties, she would entertain us with the romantic songs of her youth.

All her life she had been a housewife. "First time in years I have had a holiday like this," she would remark complacently and without a hint of self-pity.

Another person who wasn't a BCP member but had been manipulated by them was Swe, who had unknowingly delivered a letter from one BCP member to another. She was probably one of the sweetest people I have ever met in my life, considerate of others and full of compassion and humor. Even though she was the pampered only daughter of a wealthy family and had enjoyed a luxurious life, she bore no grudge against the people who had gotten her into jail. Swe had a wonderful, loving family and she was a very nurturing type; she was extremely considerate of others and cared for them lovingly and kindly.

This generosity of spirit is so often the case in Myanmar that I often marvel at my fellow countrymen. It is also due to the Theravada Buddhist concept that you suffer in this life to pay for the bad things you did in your previous life, and to improve your next one you do good in the present, although at times I think people take it too much to heart.

A person I felt honored to know was Ma Sein Pin, a poet of great talent who composed poetry in her mind and would then recite it to us. As we weren't allowed to have paper or pencils, everyone who was interested learned her poems by heart. The younger girls who were released before she was said that as soon as they got home they wrote down the poems they had memorized, and so these few works remain.

She was once a member of the underground Burma Communist Party, had lived in the jungles for about six months, and had been to prison in the late 1970s, when she had tried to overdose on sleeping pills but was found in time for her life to be saved. I didn't like her ideology at all but I loved her poems; they were beautiful and elegant, with an edgy strength.

Two years after her second release from prison, Ma Sein Pin had a stroke and now lives with her sister. She cannot write poetry anymore; her creative mind has been wiped clean and her genius is lost. I hope her collected works will be published one day but no one, not even she herself, seems to have copies of all her poems.

After January 1991, for many months I went through a bad personal time. I had learned that someone on the outside who was like my twin was dying of cancer, I couldn't get any details of his condition, and I was a miserable wreck. I was smoking nonstop and Ma Sein Pin, Pyone, Tin, and Nita, in the cell next to mine, shared their smokes with me.

Although prisoners weren't allowed to have lighters, the guards would light our cigarettes when we requested it. I would ask for a light once in the morning and from then on kept lighting my cigarettes one after the other with the stubs, chain-smoking right up until bedtime. Nita smoked only a few times during the day and got a scolding one afternoon from Mother Kyi, the grouchy elderly guard, when she asked for a light.

"You smoke too much! What, three times already today? Ma Thanegi is such a good girl, she lights up just once in the morning."

Nita shouted with laughter.

A young political prisoner named Wah Wah had a widower father whose hand in marriage she used to indiscriminately promise to anyone who would give her whatever she wanted to eat. Not that anyone actually wanted him or was even sure he was available, but the deal sounded good. Besides, people knew that with or without him as part of the deal, they would hand the food over to her anyway.

Pyone, however, was very happily married and wanted no part of this. When she gave Wah Wah some food out of the goodness of her heart, she would insist that she didn't want the father, he wasn't part of the deal.

"I didn't want her escorting him to my house in wedding finery once I'm home," she declared.

Wah Wah sold her father many times over. When I inquired how on earth he was going to handle all the women who would claim him once they were free, she dismissed it airily as his problem. I don't think he ever knew how many times he was engaged.

He was truly a good-hearted man; the Burmese believe that to drink cool coconut water during pregnancy ensures good health for the baby, and he brought Nita some from the trees in his garden every time he came to visit his daughter. Nita joked that she would be willing to keep such a nice man as a spare husband.

Among the students there was Hnin Thitsa, meaning "Snow Faithful," a very straightforward person, so earnest that she never understood when someone was messing with her as a joke and would believe whatever tall tale was being told to her. Little Sandar was petite and pretty with curly lashes and clouds of soft curly hair; she looked like a doll but her spirit was neither doll-like nor fragile. Yu Nwei was one of the happiest people we knew and her company was always welcomed, for she was never without a smile or some funny teasing comment.

A thin girl who walked like a boy was a student political prisoner we nicknamed Bei Shoke, meaning something like "Messy Duck." She was by no means messy; she just got into a lot of messy situations because of her honest streak that made her intolerant of hypocrisy in any form.

She was also intensely committed to democratic rights and fair play. She was one of the five political prisoners living in the cellblock of the other women's section who were beaten by Ma Aye Mon and transferred to Tharyarwaddy for going on strike in September 1990.

Another student of the same ilk but three times Bei Shoke's size was Tin Tin Nyo, or Nyo Gyi (Big Brown) as everyone called her. She was tall, lumbering, and unkempt, and always had a big grin on her face. Her dark eyes had a look of innocence, at times showing the pained confusion of a betrayed child.

Strong and tough, she had been badly beaten during interrogation when she refused to give up her colleagues. She denied all knowledge of their involvement and the MI couldn't break her. She used to laugh about the experience, making light of it.

Big Brown, like Messy Duck, hated fakes, hypocrites, and toadies but she was less cynical, an idealist at heart. One thing that made her furious was seeing or hearing of a lack of unity in our democratic forces at any level.

"Cowards! They're cowards, Aunty Lay," she would complain to me. "They should be fighting for our cause, not with each other."

She was unwaveringly forthright of speech, which got her into a lot of trouble both inside and outside prison; she could never understand why people prefer to believe pleasant lies rather than the painful truth. After her release in 1991 we lost touch; a few years later I heard that she committed suicide. We never learned what finally crushed her spirit when prison couldn't.

In December of 1990, on my birthday, a group of elected NLD members of parliament were imprisoned and sent to our block in the evening. Just before they arrived, Pyone and others were hurriedly told to pack their things and were moved back to the hall.

The thirty-eight MPs were later all sentenced to twenty-five years, after which they had walked out of the court, heads high and smiling. After they were sentenced, the women MPs in our cellblock were told to move to the hall. One of them, Ma Ohn, a lawyer, sat with her bags packed and cried because she had to leave us. Mother Kyi thought she was crying because of her long sentence and, being nice for once, tried to comfort her. But Ma Ohn wasn't appreciative, she was furious that Mother Kyi thought she was crying because she got twenty-five years, and she yelled at the poor old lady that she was crying because she didn't want to leave us…twenty-five years meant nothing to her, she said.

Mother Kyi, her one attempt at kindness having blown up in her face, flounced away muttering that she couldn't understand "you crazy women." Luckily the higher authorities changed their mind and Ma Ohn and the rest were allowed to remain in our cellblock, so she was soon smiling again.

Among the MPs besides Ma Ohn and her friend Ma Hlaing was Daw San San, and they all became good friends with Nita, Pyone, and me. Aunty San was a very frank person with the innocence of a child, intelligent but naïve in a way that allowed others to fool her. She was conned numerous times and she would always laugh at herself afterward, without anger or resentment. I never saw her angry.

Ma Hlaing was from a small town in Upper Myanmar, a slim, fair woman with an elegant, aristocratic beauty, brains, and a law degree. She came from an area famous all over the country for its searing wit, and just to listen to her talk was excellent entertainment for us.

Once she told us of an *Ahnyeint* dance show held in her town. The performers of this traditional genre liked to incorporate modern touches to draw crowds and this particular troupe was led by a diva called Glorious Emerald.

That was in the late 1970s, and the fashion-model culture didn't hit our society until nearly twenty years later. However, Glorious Emerald seemed to be way ahead of her time—she had a catwalk built into the audience and from that she modeled her considerable wardrobe of western evening gowns. Those in attendance were all simple and conservative country folks who had never in their lives seen anything like it.

"The first of the dresses she wore was long, almost covering her toes," Ma Hlaing recounted, "and was cut low in the back. It was emerald green of a very soft material, and she wore green stiletto heels. Her toenails were painted green, too! Did I tell you she was rather tall and very fair, with a complexion like milk? She completely bowled us over. She was a magnificent sight, Aunty Lay, can you imagine it?"

I could.

"Well then, a yokel married to one of my cousins was so fascinated he stood with his chin on the edge of the catwalk. I was on the opposite side and could see him with a glazed look on his face, and his wife sitting just behind him. Well, whenever Glorious Emerald sashayed past he would purse his lips and blow on her toes: I could see it all. My cousin didn't notice at first but when she did, she covered up her head with her shawl and began to wail, 'I am disgraced! I am disgraced! He's blowing on her toes! Mother, my dead mother, get up from your grave and see what he is doing! You promised he was a good man when you married me off to him!'

"The commotion nearly ended the show but my cousin's husband was happy, even the next day when his wife threw her pots and pans at him and ordered him out of the house. It took the abbot of our monastery, the whole family, and the town council ten days to get them back together. My, my, you couldn't say the word 'toe' to my cousin ever again."

We never tried to out-talk this woman, for she had a sharp tongue and won every debate. After her release she came to Yangon with almost nothing in her pocket, took lessons in English, and began to work for various companies. Just a year and a half later she borrowed some capital to set up her own business and was able to repay the loan in a few months. She married a handsome man who adored her and their business is doing well. Her wit remains as sharp as ever.

Ma Ohn was already married with children when she arrived in Insein. She and her strong and silent husband were farmers in Upper Myanmar. He talked so little that we were in stitches when we heard how he had courted her almost without words.

She had beautiful lustrous eyes ringed with thick dark lashes, smooth and glowing dark skin, and eyebrows like wings. She adored cats and had five of them who all had names that were as poetic and pretty as if they had been given to young girls, such as Lady Rose and Jasmine Pure. She also had two sons whom she missed a lot, but she knew her husband could handle things and raise them well, so she was unconcerned about their welfare. However, she worried about her cats.

More than we ever knew about her husband and sons, we soon knew every detail of appearance, size, age, food preferences and prejudices, particular characteristics, and family trees of Lady Rose, Jasmine Pure, and the rest. Those who hated cats couldn't avoid hearing this soft lilting voice talk about her adored kitties, all five of them; we often heard groans coming from these cells, but Ma Ohn was such a sweet person that no one had the heart to tell her to shut up. We all frequently assured her that if we ever were to meet her cats on the street we would recognize them instantly and would be able to greet each by name.

Among the students who were arrested in 1989 was the notorious Shorty, who had starred as the baby in Tin Thein's dramatic production. Her real name had a word in it which means tall, but because she was all of four feet nine inches high, we deemed her unfit for that adjective, and so she became Shorty from the very beginning.

She could make everyone helpless with laughter so she got away with a lot of mischief. When she broke any rules, the jailers or guards couldn't scold her, for as soon as they tried she made them laugh. They had to flee from her because if they told her to go away and leave them alone she would stick like a burr and crack more jokes.

When she was still living in the hall, Shorty would eye the parcels brought in by Pyone and Nita after their visitors had gone. Leading a pack of followers, she would sidle up to sweet-talk the "aunties" (who knew exactly what she was up to) into letting the gang help put away the groceries. Then, rummaging through the parcels and taking what they wanted to eat, they would leave everything in a mess and go away to pass on the news of what was available to the other kids who had not been present at this foraging mission.

Pyone and Nita were never quick enough about hiding their things— perhaps they didn't have the heart to. Every week they would fall easy prey to this daylight robbery, which they suffered with good grace.

"They're the same age as our kids," they would moan, laughing at how they had been bullied. "What can we do?"

Inside my food parcels there was a regular supply of the soft, fermented tofu made in the Shan State. It is sometimes called the cheese of the East and it is an acquired taste as it has a pungent smell. I loved it with rice or on bread and when I offered "cheese sandwiches" to my cellblock neighbors, they took eager bites, thinking they were getting cheddar. I had really thought they would like it but they immediately gagged and threw the food away.

Shorty was in our cellblock at the time and I gave one to her; after the first bite she wailed, "Help, help! Aunty Lay poisoned me! I'm dying!" I was delighted at her reaction, for we had often been at her mercy and payback was sweet. Even the guards were so used to her tricks that none of them came to see what the trouble was.

Another night while indulging in late-daydreaming, I unconsciously tapped my tin plate a few times with the handle of my toothbrush. In the silence the sound rang out clear and loud. Within seconds the night duty jailer, Daw Win Kyi, called from her bed at the far end of the block, "Shorty, stop that noise at once! I'm trying to sleep!"

Shorty wailed that she wasn't the culprit, but as everyone had heard that excuse quite often, nobody believed it. I stayed quiet for a minute and then resumed my tapping. Daw Win Kyi again screamed and Shorty again protested her innocence. I kept silent for a longer period and then tapped out a loud staccato, ending with a flourish.

Daw Win Kyi wailed in a wounded voice, "Please be quiet, I beg you, Shorty! My migraine's killing me!"

I stopped after that, stifling my laughter while Shorty almost in (fake) tears protested it wasn't she, that it was Aunty Lay, "out to get her." Nobody believed her, then or now.

Those were the only times I ever got the better of the Great Shorty, who was later replaced by an equally unquenchable spirit.

Soon after Shorty's sentence was over and she was released, a group of girl students was arrested and housed in the cellblock. Among them was Tiny, a lovely, dainty girl who looked like a porcelain doll but who had a scathing wit and a talent for composing mournful songs about missing home and mother. Her great sense of mischief belied her fragile looks. Several times a week there would be a cry echoing through our cellblock, "Tiny!!! Wait until I get my hands on you!"

Tiny and her group regarded amiable, plump Aunty Hpaw as being no more threatening than a fat fly. They even got around the mean-minded guard we called Chili Pepper, who stayed as far away as she could from them because she had no retort to their wit that stung as much as her "chili" did.

When the wooden walls in our cellblock were being replaced by bricks, we weren't allowed to stay in our cells while the men prisoners were working; we could sit outside almost all day. One morning, the girl students, led by Tiny, began their prank of grabbing our coffee cups when we weren't looking and drinking up half before letting us have them again. For a couple of days they had been successfully ambushing others with great glee. The older victims didn't mind really, although there were the usual screams of wait-till-I-get-you.

I usually finished my black, sugarless, and extremely strong coffee before being let out but when I saw what was happening, I brought my mug with me to sip while I ambled around, while pretending to guard it jealously. The girls' eyes lit up when they saw me enjoying my coffee with a blissful look on my face. They poked each other and watched me while I peeked at them from the corner of my eyes.

When I "carelessly" left my mug on a ledge Tiny pounced on it with glee and drank it down. Immediately she spat it back out, wailing, "Aunty Lay, what is this?" while rushing to rinse the taste from her mouth.

After that, Tiny and her comrades never stole our coffee again but they thought up many other tricks.

My small and rare victories over Shorty and Tiny were applauded by my friends, and I still take pride in these great achievements. But to my one trick each, they must have played a hundred on us.

Nobody could ever say who made more mischief, Shorty or Tiny. The two of them were legends of our time in Insein and together they would have caused more havoc than anyone could handle. Each time the guards had to deal with Tiny's pranks, they would often groan, thanking God that Shorty's jail time didn't coincide with Tiny's.

7. THE GUARDS

The guards at first treated us political prisoners with suspicion and alarm, since up until our arrival they had no experience with women from good families who weren't criminals, or poor, or uneducated. Gradually they began to know us and became friendly but the one thing none of them did was to help in anything political.

Most were in their thirties or forties, the wives of guards, ordinary women, not highly educated, with narrow lives that involved only their work and their families. Others were much older, uneducated, due for retirement, and very conservative. The few in their twenties with university degrees were smarter and more observant of prison rules and discipline than their older colleagues.

Prisoners preferred jailers who took their job seriously (for that meant that at least they took responsibility when things needed to be done), along with the ones who cared about the welfare of their charges within the rules.

Granted, there weren't a great number of this breed, but there were some. They were the ones who made sure that prisoners had enough mats to sleep on, that bedbugs were killed off on a regular schedule, and that mothers and children received the blankets they were entitled to in cold weather, along with their special supplemental food and medication. These were the better sorts of women jailers and guards I met during my stay.

Most women in jail, prisoners or guards, were just humans trying to get through life, struggling with low incomes, marital problems, and worry for their children. As they said to each other, "It's a woman's lot." Only the fact that the majority of inmates had committed criminal acts, and probably would go on committing them, set them apart from people in normal society.

Most of the guards had the Myanmar spirit of being not overly strict, and apart from a few, they were quite compassionate and friendly. The two nasty ones were a very corrupt jailer called Daw Khin Mya and the guard whom we nicknamed Chili Pepper. Chili, in spite of a mean disposition, adored babies and was quite kind to new mothers, but her malicious remarks aimed at everyone apart from Daw Khin Mya made her very unpopular among both guards and prisoners.

Months after I left, the two of them were accused of corruption by some prisoners who had gathered proof of the charge. Both of them were fired and Daw Khin Mya ended up in prison herself. She wasn't the only jailer who could be bribed, not to break important prison rules but to obtain small but necessary things like tatting bobbins, nail polish, lipstick, a few extra cigarettes, or medication needed in cases of emergency. She however provided even more for prisoners who could afford her services—giving them rice of high quality that she steamed in her office with a rice cooker or sending and delivering daily letters. She also put pressure on those who couldn't or wouldn't pay her and that I felt was her biggest crime.

Everyone hated her, especially after she appointed pickpocket Daw Kyee Gan (Madame Crow) the *Tan Zee* or monitor-in-charge for the downstairs hall where the poor criminals lived. Daw Kyee Gan, a very dark, fat, sleazy woman, demanded a lot of bribes for things that she had the authority to allot, such as the best sleeping areas next to the French windows. She was cruel to people who couldn't pay her in the prison tender of cheroots. As she was in the downstairs hall, she had no jurisdiction over the political prisoners who lived upstairs, where there was a Tan Zee of a better nature and class. The Tan Zee were rotated so there was usually a change every three months or so but Daw Khin Mya kept Madame Crow in power for a long time.

Ma Cho was one of the nicer guards, although her voice was extremely loud, and harsh enough to blister your eardrums. When she screamed at someone we could practically see the sound waves flying through the air. When the vagrant girls begged her for some nga pi yay she would call them names but the next day would bring them some with nasty remarks, which no one minded—it was all for show.

A strict disciplinarian, Ma Cho had few problems with the convicts. She was furious when the wily ones fawned over her. "Don't fawn! You toady! Get away from me!" she would shout and push them away. Some vagrants, bored with nothing to do, would flatter Ma Cho deliberately so that they could laugh, from a safe distance, at her colorful and very loudly screamed language. She herself never toadied to anyone and it was one thing that drove her wild.

Ma Kyu was a guard with a fiery temper but a good heart. She would scream with outrage at any unfairness, even from jailers. If things got too bad at home or at work, she would sob like a big child. Happily married when she was seventeen, she was widowed at twenty-one with a young son to care for after her husband died of cerebral malaria. She then married an older man, a jailer, short-tempered but kind, who loved her and usually gave in to her every wish. He had been a firm but loving father to her son until relatives meddled, causing antagonism between the two and a lot of worry for Ma Kyu.

One summer evening, when she came in for night duty she passed me a present, a bunch of the earliest *padauk* flowers. Padauk blooms but once a year in April when the spring showers fall just before the Water Festival. Tiny, fluffy, golden yellow flowers, they bloom in such thick clusters that no leaves or branches can be seen on the trees bearing the blossoms and their fragrance is utterly refreshing, sweet, and romantic. During their brief season, which lasts only a few days, when we caught their scent in the air, we would stand at our windows, sniffing like bird dogs.

The guards often tucked flowers into their coiled hair when they came on duty and then would distribute them among the inmates. We badly missed the flowers that announced each new season—padauk, of course; the *gant-gaw*, a flower that looks like a sunny-side-up egg with its own unique perfume; gardenias, fat and creamy; lush roses in the cool season; jasmine in the rain.

Guard Daw Pyu wore her hair in a large bun, where she would hide a few green chilies to give to the Rakhine inmates who couldn't eat rice without the heat of chili. Another guard, Ma Nwei, loved movies and would act out the stories for us while standing up straight, almost at attention. When I finally saw one box-office hit she had told us, it was nowhere near as good as the one I saw in my mind while listening to her.

Ah Moe, which in Karen means "mother," was what we called one middle-aged guard with a dry wit, a levelheaded perspective, and the strength to survive a hard life with a sick husband, useless children, and debts. She was considerate and highly intelligent, not lacking in either IQ or EQ, although she had left school in fifth grade.

One Karen guard was adored by everyone from inmates and jailers (with the exception of the corrupt Daw Khin Mya) to guards. Even Chili Pepper loved her. Daw Shwe Hmone, "Madame Gold Dust," was her name but everyone called her Naw Naw, which I think means "elder sister" in Karen. If anyone was unfit to be a prison guard, and yet was better at the job than anyone else, it was this lady.

She was about fifty-six when I first met her, only four feet six inches tall, skinny as a little girl, with fair skin and sparkling dark eyes in a small oval face. She had a sweet voice that soothed us when she was the one to pray aloud before bedtime. We begged her to sit and pray where we could all hear her, even tough and cynical Daw Myint Myint Khin who thought Naw Naw was a saint.

She would kneel in the middle of our aisle and say her special prayer softly but audibly. I have forgotten the exact words, but it was a mixture of traditional Buddhist chants and the Christian Lord's Prayer, full of goodwill and love to all creatures. What I remember is one sentence at the end: "May those who are wrongly sent to prison be released as soon as possible. May those who are guilty regret their crimes. Lord, look after them as well as you do everyone, and put repentance in their hearts."

With her gentleness she could control anyone in any situation, even when vagrants fought in a free-for-all crowd with no one remembering who was on whose side. In such cases the other guards were reluctant to go in, because when blind with fury, the combatants would bash anyone up well and good first and answer for it later. Once when a group of Thirty Ds got into a brawl, clawing at one another's faces, Naw Naw simply waded into the mêlée waving a bamboo stick that was taller than she was. From our cellblock we could hear her squeaking, "Stop it! Stop it!"

When the Thirty Ds finally noticed her in their midst, as small as a child, brandishing her stick, they all stopped fighting, picked her up, and marched around the yard singing and tossing her to each other like a doll. We could hear Naw Naw's treble from beyond the metal fence: "Put me down! Put me down, at once!"

It was no small thing that maddened Thirty Ds wanted to tease her so much that they forgot their anger.

Naw Naw was the only one who could control the much-feared Aye Thida, a prostitute who had been in Insein three or four times. During each stint she made the guards and other inmates suffer more than she did. She was perhaps half-mad but had the craftiness of the insane, and she was sane enough to know when not to look mad so she never landed in the mental asylum. Or maybe the asylum refused to have her.

After once nearly killing two other inmates, she was locked up in the cell next to mine. I thought she might crash through the double wooden walls, so great was her legendary strength. We begged the jailer to please have mercy on us and let her out; she was soon released because she made enough racket to keep everyone awake all night.

In daylight she was quite chatty. She told me she had a special design of a charm in the form of an ogre tattooed on her scalp which, in her own words, "gave the power and strength of an ogre, as well as a need for sex that was uncontrollably wild or if thwarted, extremely wild." She said the last as if she regretted it but there wasn't a thing she could do—it was the charm's fault, not hers.

I could see the tattoo through the slits between the planks as she shoved her head against them and parted her hair. And she was wild, although the word "wild" seemed tame when applied to Aye Thida. As to the need for sex, she confessed that after a term in jail, usually three months, she must, must, must on the day of her release enjoy up to twenty men without asking them to pay. Ma Aye Mon the guard muttered to me, "Good luck to those fools; she probably eats them right after they have sex with her."

It scandalized the other prostitutes who saw sex as a business. They thought Aye Thida was wasting her assets.

Her temper tantrums were legendary. She was the woman who was the most often punished by being locked up in a cell and fed thin gruel instead of rice, an extreme measure of punishment. She wasn't even allowed a basin for a toilet as was the standard issue. Sand was piled in a corner like a cat box for her, because on a previous occasion she had thrown the contents of her basin in Chili Pepper's face. Both inmates and guards were delighted by this offense, which was before my time, but people still spoke of it with glee. I believe that was the only time Aye Thida received food and small gifts from the guards.

On the days when news came in that Aye Thida had been sentenced instead of fined, which she could well have afforded, both jailers and prisoners would first groan in dismay and then roundly curse the poor judge.

"Oh, damn that judge! He's sending in Aye Thida again!" the guards would cry and then would add bitterly and rather unfairly: "Let's see him take her home for just one day and see how he likes it."

Actually Aye Thida didn't come in as often as the other prostitutes; I only met her once, when she was in for three months. I suppose some judges had been warned, or perhaps the police left her alone; she had the strength of the insane, and could bite and kick like a hellion.

There were threats from other sources regarding her capture. After Aye Thida was released, Ma Aye Mon said to me that she would personally go look for and slap the lights out of the next policeman who arrested her. Probably she also announced it at the police stations when she went on her rounds of taking prisoners to the courts, for I never saw Aye Thida again. Ma Aye Mon was loud and sassy enough to be known in all police stations as someone you didn't mess with. She was also rather strong and when any hard punishment had to be done, it was she who wielded the cane.

Aye Thida could sometimes be sweet-talked into behaving herself, or she would sometimes sweet-talk people who looked as though they could be useful to her. Then she would be demure, polite, and charming, until the next time someone accidentally upset her.

She knew we weren't poor so, to us in the cellblock, or to Tin, Pyone, and others in the hall, she would be very sweet, saying "Goota maaawnin" (her version of good morning) to us, calling us Marmie, and cadging cigarettes. We handed them over hastily, not prepared to give offense to She Who Was Feared by All.

The jailers usually distanced themselves from her as they could never be sure that, unprovoked, she wouldn't let loose with a string of highly imaginative and colorful obscenities right there in front of everyone. Besides, lashings with bamboo or cane left her unconcerned and apparently unhurt.

Aye Thida could only be handled by Naw Naw, She of the Pure Heart. Once I saw her cuddled up on Naw Naw's lap like a kitten because that lady had promised to bring some home-cooked beef curry, her favorite dish. (On Thursday meat ration times, one guard had to follow Aye Thida around at a safe distance in case she knocked over someone to steal a piece of beef.)

The jailers of each of the two women's sections went to great lengths to get Naw Naw assigned to their compound, even going to the wives of the highest authorities with bags of apples or with cake to beg them for some pillow-talk lobbying on their behalf. However, Naw Naw was assigned to each compound fairly, for even the highest officials knew her worth and wouldn't interfere in the case of this prison saint. She and her husband retired around 1995 and I heard they went back to their village near Pa-an, capital of the Kayin State.

Another guard who was also a favorite of inmates and other guards, although not one who could match Naw Naw, was the one in charge of health care: Aunty Hpaw, or "Aunty Flower," who had a health assistant's diploma. Three times heavier than Naw Naw, she was perhaps two inches taller. Tease her for five minutes, and fat tears would roll down her even fatter cheeks. Wheedle her enough and she would blushingly recount how she met her husband of twenty years, how he stole a kiss, and what her father did to her for that, getting teary at the tragic parts of not being allowed to see her sweetheart for two weeks until they eloped.

Aunty Hpaw was a motherly soul, but prone to bursting into tears at the slightest provocation. Prisoners and guards liked to tease her to the point of tears and then hug and console her. It was like hugging a gigantic bolster.

From what she told us, she had a very loving large family, all of them working hard to grow vegetables, raise a cow to sell milk, and fatten a few pigs for the market. She kept us up-to-date on how fat her pigs were getting and how her kids were doing in school. She would often tell the criminals about her family, "so that they might think it's a good idea to work hard and not go around stealing things," as she explained to us, but I doubt if it worked at all. The dedicated criminals I met seemed quite happy in their chosen professions.

One young guard, Thida Oo, a shy Karen woman, worked to get a college degree by correspondence course, which she did just before I was released, to great jubilation all around.

Once, a guard back from court duty brought in a pair of shiny handcuffs while I was walking outside my block and left them on the office table. Just to see if it were possible to get out of them, for I have narrow hands and who knew if I might need to use the trick one day, I cuffed myself on both wrists. Thida Oo and Aunty Hpaw who were sitting nearby went pale, appalled that I had done something "inauspicious," that people in Myanmar avoid at all costs. They gave chase while I skipped away saying, "Just a minute! Just a minute!" while not letting them see that I was trying to slip my hands through.

I couldn't do it and I never saw a pair of handcuffs again. Afterward Aunty Hpaw gave me a scolding about not tempting the fates with bad omens, although I argued that I was already in prison if she cared to notice, and how much worse could my fate be?

During the week of the Water Festival in the heat of April, the student prisoners in the hall wanted to give away cups of a traditional dessert of the season to their friends and the poor inmates, as it is the custom to share desserts during the festivities. They had the necessary condensed milk, rose syrup, and sugar but they needed bits of jelly and ice. It was Thida Oo who brought in jelly bits plus a large piece of ice, big enough to cool, if not chill, this offering.

On special occasions such as birthdays or to commemorate death anniversaries of loved ones, some of us made merit by donating food to the poorer inmates. For this we would give a guard or two some money through our families to bring us fresh noodles, stir-fried vegetables, some sliced fried sausages, and omelets (or we would use our hoarded supply of hard-boiled eggs). We would mix the first three ingredients with some light soy sauce and garlic-infused oil sent from home, put a serving in a fresh plastic bag sent in by our families, garnish it with shreds of omelets or slices of hard-boiled eggs, and there we had "fried" noodles. The jailer would call the poorer inmates, normally about two hundred of them, to stand in a line and with the help of our friends we would distribute the small bags. Many guards were happy to help with the merit making.

Ma Aye Mon, buxom and loud, had a computerlike brain that remembered almost everyone who passed through while she was there. She acted tough, but was fair-minded. However, this didn't mean she hesitated in dealing out punishment. The five young women political prisoners transferred to Tharyarwaddy Prison for demonstrating in Insein had been beaten by her.

If you got on her bad side by trying to pull a fast one, she would make your life miserable. She was ruthless if crossed or cheated but if you confided in her about needing contraband such as hair dye, lipsticks, or nail polish, she would help (although never with paper and pens, which could be used for political purposes).

She handled the office work with Thida Oo as her assistant. For many months I was in a cell with the window overlooking her desk and had the leisure to watch her at work.

All new prisoners needed to be registered, which meant they had to squat in rows while Ma Aye Mon called out their names from the list given to her by the justice department. The prisoners then came forward and stated their names, their father's names, and their addresses to be checked against the registration list.

Once I heard her bark at a woman: "You, I remember you from two years ago and your father's name was different then. Are you trying to fool me?" The prisoner admitted the name she just supplied was false.

She told us about her family, proudly showing us the photo of her pretty younger sister in high school. "She's too pretty," she said dryly. "I make sure that if I'm not available our mother walks with her to and from school. I don't like guys hanging around her."

She herself had married when still in the eighth grade. She was divorced soon after the birth of her son. "I cannot allow my sister to become like me," she said.

Fiercely devoted to her aging parents, she was the one who held the family together, making sure her two younger sisters and one brother went to school regularly.

"I know how easy it is to be led into a life of crime," she said grimly. "I won't let it happen to them if it kills me or I kill them."

Mother Kyi, whom we loved to torment, was known for being stubborn. One night we heard a cat mewing and when we excitedly asked her its color, she replied quite seriously, "Sea green." That was the only color, we firmly told her, that cats were incapable of being. She sniffed, nose in the air, and wouldn't budge from her stand however hard we pressured her.

Daw Win Kyi, with a pretty smile and lovely eyes, was a jailer who unfortunately had an overly romantic turn of mind. When she was seventeen she became infatuated with a good-looking, older man who already had a wife and grown-up children. She chased him, got herself pregnant, and married him. He was nice enough to her, but what she wanted was romance, and didn't care much about looking after the two children she had with him, a boy and girl. The kids were perpetually dirty, underfed, and not very healthy; they were usually dumped at her sister's house while she gadded about flirting with other men, single or married. She loved reading cheap romances and would tell us the stories, her eyes shining. It was evident that she identified with the heroines.

She kept having affairs with other men and getting into messy situations. The men usually passed her on to others when she got too clingy. If a man was nice to her, she would immediately assume that he was falling for her.

After a stint as a jailer for our side she was transferred to the other side. One day some weeks after that, a prisoner's husband, a wealthy, good-looking man, had to ask Daw Win Kyi's help to get urgent medication to his sick wife in an emergency. Out of gratitude he gave her a present, which is a normal courtesy.

She fell for the husband, and would often visit the ill wife to tell her about her imagined romance of how he had looked deep into her eyes or tried to touch her hand, etc. The wife, knowing her husband well, was simply amused by the lies and ignored them.

When I finally heard about this, I decided it had gone on long enough. The wife was a very decent, classy woman, in jail not for committing a crime but getting swept up in someone else's mess. I passed on a message through Aunty Flower, loud enough to be overheard by several guards, that if Daw Win Kyi ever came into our compound again I would slap her silly and *then* tell the authorities why.

If the whole story came out it would have been worse for her, attacked by a detainee who was supposed to be in isolation and who had no business knowing what she was up to, so she never came over to harass the wife again. My cellblock was right by the gate, and I kept an eagle eye on it. Once she came to the gate and stood talking to Aunty Hpaw but didn't come in. I stood with folded arms where she could see me and stared icily at her the whole time. It wasn't a long chat.

A month or so after that someone in our cellblock had a tummyache late at night, and our jailer was off while Daw Win Kyi from the other side was on night duty. As she was also responsible for our section that night, she came into our cellblock with the male doctor, calling out loudly, "I am here only on duty! I am here only on duty!"—no doubt being sarcastic for my benefit, but I was grinning in my cell. Gotcha, I thought.

A few years after I was released I heard that she left her children with a relative and eloped with the eighteen-year-old son of a wealthy prisoner in her charge. After six months, the young man left her when she got pregnant. She quit her job or was fired. I heard that no one, including her previous husband and children, found out what became of her or her baby.

The last jailer we had, Daw Aye Aye Than, was very considerate; she was the best of the five I met. Most of the prisoners who had known the other jailers really appreciated her kindness to all, especially the poor. She was always careful about our health, tasting the rice before the delivery men left. If she found it was undercooked, she would send it back to the kitchen in exchange for a better batch.

Not only did she not harass the prisoners, but she would bring her own stuff and her children's castoffs to share with children and mothers as well as poorer prisoners. She kept bringing her husband's worn-out longyi to give to new mothers so they could tear them into diapers and she said her husband had taken to hiding his clothing because it kept disappearing so often. The old longyi, worn and soft, are the most comfortable to wear around the house and he preferred them to the new ones she offered to buy for him.

Some mothers ate the nutrition ration of chicken and gruel that was meant for their children, or would exchange it for cheroots. Daw Aye Aye Than kept these mothers and kids by her desk at mealtimes so she could make sure the mothers fed them all of their allotted food. Prisoners often gave the guards gifts of packets of biscuits or sweets from their parcels, but Daw Aye Aye Than would instantly give her presents away to the poor.

8. THINGS WITH FEATHERS

I had no family to miss except my dog Bibi. My friend Liz had given her to me when she was the size of a tennis ball and was as white, round, and fuzzy as one. She had immediately snuggled in the palm of my hand, fast asleep with eyes tightly shut. She was then only days old and I took her home after two months. She grew up small, with a pretty and neat nose, black eyes that were either mischievous or sulky, and soft white fur. She had a patch of orange and black over one eye and her tail was fluffy, at times whirling like a fan.

She was all bravado and liked to pretend to chase my landlady's cat but when he turned on her hissing in fury, Bibi would run into our house, yelping in terror. She slept next to me, head on her own pillow. She had the run of the tiny house we shared but one thing she wasn't allowed to do was beg when I was eating. This annoyed her so much that at mealtimes she would sit with her back to me, resentment apparent in every bristling hair, making a statement of protest against my cruelty.

Some months after I began to work with Ma Suu, I moved into one large room in a cousin's house so that when I traveled, Bibi could be looked after. My cousin Ma Ma Htay and her five children loved dogs and had several, but they spoiled Bibi so much that soon, to my horror, she was eating at their table. When they thought she was under the weather, they made chicken noodle soup for her. When she played in the rain with the other dogs, she, the only pet allowed indoors, would track mud and water all over the highly polished floors and no one was allowed to scold her, including me. Once when I gave her a few pats on her fat little rump for trying to rip apart a silk cushion from their parlor, the whole family nearly cried and comforted Bibi for an hour while pouting at me. Now she lived with them permanently.

Imprisoned animal lovers miss the comfort that comes from a warm, furry pet cuddling next to them; I certainly missed Bibi and longed for the companionship of a friendly animal. Then I received a sparrow.

He came into my life within the first few months after my arrival in 1989, during a raging monsoon. A nest had blown down in the storm and the girl who cleaned my cellblock brought me a naked baby bird, which I put in a plastic cup lined with a handkerchief to keep warm. It looked disgusting, with a wobbly, translucent tummy, big yellow beak, and tightly closed eyes.

Years before, I had raised a couple of baby sparrows when they fell out of their nest and had learned then that to get a baby bird to open its beak, the mother bird must give it a nudge on its forehead. Now I gave this baby a tap with my fingertip on his forehead and it immediately opened its beak wide, eyes still shut. I shoved in some chewed food I had ready in my other hand and from that point on we were in business. It thrived, and since baby birds need to be fed very, very often, I was kept happily busy tending to this one's needs. I called him Twee, short for Tweety Bird, who with his friend Sylvester was the favorite cartoon character of my childhood.

As he grew I came to think of Twee as masculine because he was so possessive and demanding. He was distinctive, with a pale cream underside, and lighter feathers on his upper body than other sparrows, which we thought was because he grew up away from the sun. He often pooped down my back while sitting on my shoulder so I had to change my blouse several times a day.

At weekly jailer visits, I kept him hidden under a shelter I made for him, a large plastic basin with airholes that I had burned through with a lit cigarette. He slept under this too, perched on a stick inserted in two cross-holes. When I went out to bathe or to take my daily exercise, I had to leave him under his basin to keep him safe from mice. He would chatter with relief and annoyance on my return, bending down to nibble my thumb as he sat on my forefinger.

My cellblock mates were all charmed with Twee and even the guards would rush to greet him as soon as they came in for their shifts. If I was napping during the day he would perch on my hipbone while I lay on my side. From there he would shriek in fury at any face appearing at the opening in the door. Anybody who looked in on us on their walks or on their way to bathe always got scolded by Twee.

He walked about my cell or clung to my clothes, for he hated to let me out of his sight, and probably had no idea of how to fly; he had never seen anyone or anything flying. We all worried that he was going to spend his whole life walking. When he wanted a bath, which was often during the hot season, he would tweak my thumb. Then I had to fill a basin with cool water, and holding him loosely in my fingers I would swish him back and forth. He always looked pleased after this, his beak opened slightly in what looked like a silly grin.

When he wanted to go to bed at night, he would peck his basin and nip my hand. He never went to bed at twilight; his bedtime was mostly after taps. He got up around 8 a.m; he was no early bird.

After he grew more feathers, I noticed that his tail feathers weren't growing straight and was worried that this might prevent him from flying well. So, apologizing to him and agonizing on his behalf, I plucked them out over the course of a few days. It must have been painful; he jumped and looked at me with a startled expression as each one was pulled out. Afterward I fed him cod liver oil from capsules I broke and squeezed into his beak while keeping him on his back so he couldn't spit it out. His tail feathers soon grew back, straight and strong. He also became rather big with the food he received at all hours of the day and night.

Parcel days were a treat. He was a messy eater and he ate everything I did, perching on my left hand, which held the plate while I fed him with my right. He shrieked if there was the slightest delay so he had to be fed first. He would chew greedily, a look of great satisfaction on his face with food dripping out of his beak, which he would wipe on the back of my hand.

He loved soft-cooked corn and creamed candy; he liked flakes of fish. He would spit out bread if it wasn't buttered and sprinkled with sugar. He loved shreds of chicken (white meat only) and cake, and he swallowed noodles as if they were worms. He also liked hard-boiled egg yolks, although I felt uneasy feeding a bird hard-boiled eggs even though they were from chickens and not sparrows. Every time I received special food in my parcel such as a few chocolates or a cream puff, I would give him some. When someone shared half a cup of Coke with me, I gave Twee a few drops. He loved it, smacking his beak appreciatively. He always spat out what he didn't like; he hated plain rice and wouldn't eat one single grain if it weren't mixed with a little gravy or sugar.

At leisure he would sit on my knee or forefinger and chatter incessantly, looking up into my face. Or he would sit on my shoulder and twitter into my ear. He uttered long monologues with expressive tones in his chirps as he argued and made his points. I had to listen and respond, Oh yes, really? Is that so?—much the same way I used to at cocktail parties when cornered by boring men, but Twee was definitely more charming than any of them had been. If I didn't make appropriate replies he would nip my ear or finger.

Even while he talked, he would often decide to take a nap midspeech and would do so, tucking his head under a wing, waking up a minute later to resume his monologue. It always gave a lift of joy to my heart that he trusted me enough to go to sleep while perched on my finger.

He loved to be kissed on his belly, which was the only space wide enough for my nose as I breathed in the downy smell of his soft feathers. When I did that his eyes would sparkle and his beak would open wide in a grin.

News of Twee spread quickly, and all the baby birds found out of their nests were immediately brought to my window. Most of the other baby sparrows that were given to me were deformed one way or the other, sometimes with feet turned inward, or born without wings. During hot summers, baby birds sometimes hatched with deformed feet, which meant they couldn't make the strong leap necessary to take off in flight. After waiting for some time the mother birds would push the crippled ones out of the nest, to make room for those that would survive.

After raising a few baby birds, I discovered a surprising fact: that each of these small creatures has a different face and personality. They could think. *Birdbrain* is a term not applicable to sparrows.

The sparrows came and went; some flew away, some were killed by mice or died of illness. Twee, who lived with me over six months, the longest of all, was insanely jealous of every single bird he met. It kept me busy just to see that he didn't get a chance to sit on their backs and tear off their heads with his beak, something he tried often enough. If I had to go out for exercise or baths, I dared not leave Twee loose or he would have killed them all. Fortunately, none came in as young as Twee had been so it was easier to look after them and protect them from his murderous intentions. I had a few separate plastic basins to house all of them, Twee of course apart from others.

One baby that Twee disliked but not enough to injure was a charming little bird with a round face I called Sweet, for she looked very feminine, hopping about, fluffing her feathers, and chirping softly to herself. She really was a quiet, sweet-tempered little bird. She flew off before she was full-grown, and was instantly snatched away by a crow as soon as she got into the air. I can still hear her screams. I often wished it were possible to tell the sparrows that it was dangerous to fly before they were really strong.

One bird came in with a large open wound on his head. I thought he would die, and I wanted to put him out of his misery. Everyone, including the nasty guard Chili Pepper and the prisoners who were in for murder, refused to snap his neck when I asked. They even refused to listen to my speeches about euthanasia and how it was "for the best to stop his pain." They were all horrified at my request.

I finally had to cajole a couple of sleeping pills out of the health assistant Aunty Hpaw. I told her I wasn't sleeping well and that at home I often took two Valium tablets to get to sleep. Actually it took me five but I knew she wouldn't give me that many, and I was sure two would be enough to put one small sparrow to eternal sleep.

Afraid I was going to commit suicide, Aunty Hpaw wouldn't give me any until I howled at her, "No one can die from taking two Valium, for God's sake." She gave in reluctantly; I crushed the tablets to powder and mixed them into some food which I fed to the wounded sparrow.

He didn't die; he snored for two days in a little plastic cup lined with a hanky. He woke up looking chirpy and ate everything I fed him, but he didn't recover from his wound. One day he suddenly dropped his head on his chest and expired.

Another special sparrow I loved was Cassidy, who was born with good feet but without wing feathers; they wouldn't grow even though I dosed him with cod liver oil. I called him Cassidy because he hopped along happily, being friendly. He was very kind and liked to give moral support to other baby birds by sitting close to them, chirping softly and giving gentle tweaks at their cheek feathers as if giving kisses. He kept well away from Twee, who retaliated against his friendly gestures with murderous glares, beady eyes flashing pure hatred. I loved Cassidy, to Twee's jealous fury.

Cassidy's constant companion was Sar U (Sparrow Egg), which is a typical yokel's name. He was a very dumb, slow little bird with his large beak perpetually wide open, giving him the look of a village idiot. He stuck close to Cassidy, for even though he was stupid, he knew enough to stay away from Twee, who detested as well as scorned him. I thought I could actually see a sneer on Twee's face when he spotted Sar U.

Once I had a very nervous and wild mynah bird baby, who screamed in a far corner near the loo basin. Cassidy and Sar U went over to sit close to him in that corner, where they normally never went at all. They seemed to be trying to calm down the agitated bird, who was ten times bigger than they, by giving small chirps from time to time and trying to sit close to him. Without Cassidy I am sure Sar U would never have gone near that alarming creature—even I avoided him and nourished him only by throwing food into his corner. Finally after a few days of agitated shrieking and panic the mynah grew strong enough to fly away. Cassidy and Sar U, with looks of relief on their faces, came away from that corner and never went there again. It was obvious that Cassidy deliberately went there to be a comfort to the mynah and Sar U as usual had followed him.

On cold nights, I would often take the birds into my jacket to allow them to sleep in the warmth of my neck. One evening I was dozing with my face to the wall just before taps, when I heard small chirps coming from behind my back. Twee was already asleep under his basin. I rolled over to see Cassidy, with walleyed Sar U by his side, both looking up at me. They were standing very close to each other and they exchanged a quick glance when they saw they had my attention. Then Cassidy began to chirp urgently at me; I pulled them into my neck under my collar, and they promptly settled down to sleep.

Cassidy was taken by a mouse while I was out of the room and had forgotten to put him under the protection of a basin. Of course he couldn't fly to get away. Sar U died of fever soon after.

When Twee grew old enough I was careful to keep the windows closed while teaching him to fly. I didn't willingly set him free, although he had a free run of my cell and the windows were always open. He seemed to have no interest in going outside, but one afternoon he flew away while I was busy with a few baby sparrows that he had tried to kill that morning. I had scolded him and I think he left in a snit. I was in a frenzy of despair, as were my friends and others who knew him.

Everyone, including the guards, felt miserable and worried about how he would survive. My friends from the other cells and from the hall would often come to voice their worries over Twee: Who would he talk to? Would he even know sparrow language? How would he fit into bird life? He slept until eight in the morning! What would he eat? He hated plain rice! He liked creamed candy; where would he find any?

Two weeks after he disappeared, Ma Nwei, the nice guard, came in for her shift early one morning and immediately came to my door; she was very excited. The previous day she had gone with her young son to the local grocery to buy rice. While the boy was playing in front of the store, a rather big sparrow with the coloring of pale beige just like Twee had lighted on his fingers and stayed for a few minutes. Twee had very pale feathers and certainly, a wild sparrow wouldn't come that close to a human or stay so long.

I felt so relieved. If he had survived two weeks in the wide world, he must not be doing too badly. Ma Nwei said there was a monastery nearby: she hoped Twee lived in that compound, for then he would be safe from kids carrying catapults.

Altogether I must have raised about twenty-five sparrows. Sometimes as I looked at my feathered pets, I would think of a book I had read in my youth, about the Birdman of Alcatraz, a lifer in a maximum-security prison of the United States who had studied birds. A lifer! Not a very fortunate role model for me, I would groan to myself.

I still love to remember one late night when I was lost in thought, as I sat leaning against a wall with Twee perched on my hand. Either he was in a foul mood or he wanted a snack because he was pecking rather hard at my fingers. Still lost in reverie I didn't at once attend to his needs but muttered to him, "Stop, darling, don't do that! Ow, it hurts! Stop it now!"

From the next cell there came a quivering little voice asking, "Gi Gi, who exactly are you calling darling?"

Nita thought I had somehow smuggled in a man.

9. PRISON TALES

Men certainly were missing in our lives. A few vagrant women, petty criminals, or prostitutes acted butch just so that they would receive favors such as food or pampering from those who, as the guards said, "wanted a whiff of fake testosterone."

I was eager to get to know members of the whole Thirty D criminal society, for in the outside world there was no way I could get a chance to get chummy with them.

Some of my artist friends were poor and some weren't, and a few had slept in the streets, not because they were homeless but because they were drunk. So I was used to associating with all levels of society and could easily move from one to the other. I could fit in anywhere, like a stray puppy who can make a home in any hut or garbage dump.

In Insein I was most eager to talk to pickpockets, to learn their trade if I could (it would be useful if I wanted to play a joke on my friends and might perhaps provide a lucrative career when I was released), and to ask prostitutes and vagrants about their lives.

My friends in the hall once gave some cheroots to a vagrant to sweep their floor and were amazed when she didn't even know how to handle the broom; she was pushing it on the ground, Tin told me, and not doing sweeping motions. She said she then realized that of course, vagrants had never lived in a house with floors they could sweep.

Vagrants, prostitutes, and petty criminals were in and out of prison so regularly that they often joked it was like coming home. When some were released after the usual three- month sentence, those left behind for longer terms would tell them to bring them a special snack next time they returned.

The elderly women who were addicted to gambling and sentenced for playing poker would say, even to the jailers, that they'd be happy to spend their whole life in Insein as long as they received regular food parcels and had a deck of cards. That drove the jailers wild.

Prostitutes wouldn't even glance at men who came to our compound as officers, doctors, electricians, or inmates carrying bags of rice, unlike some other women who liked to enjoy the sight of something they missed a lot. To the hookers, men were nothing more than customers.

Brothels often hired a poor elderly woman to act as manager or owner and when the police raided the bordellos, she would confess to being the madam and be the one charged and convicted. She would be assured of a regular food parcel on family visits while the real owner would hire another like her to take her place. These women were usually without families to look after them; they didn't have anything to do but serve other people's jail terms.

There was one prostitute in her forties who was said to have three daughters, each of whom she had sold to an upscale brothel for a huge virgin price. In prison society, inmates know who did what, and nobody would be her friend, not even the other prostitutes, who might sell themselves but never their children.

A group of prostitutes, of a higher echelon than the streetwalkers (who were often in jail for earning just twenty kyat for a quickie in an alley), came in with a group of women who smuggled goods from Thailand, illegally crossing the border. Each of the prostitutes had given the smugglers 30,000 kyat to take them into Thailand where they could make more money. All were caught and sentenced to three years for human trafficking, which made the smugglers quite indignant. As they pointed out, "They paid *us* money to take *them!*"

A businesswoman named Hein, with her husband and a few government employees whom they had bribed, were all sentenced to twenty-five years apiece for smuggling a huge ruby from Hein's mine in Mogok to Thailand. They had made the sale and were counting their bales of money in a hotel room when the police raided them. The ruby, which was of an excellent quality and color, weighing over five hundred carats, was recovered and confiscated by the government. Named the Nawata Ruby, it remains a state treasure.

Hein still had her license to operate her mine for two more years and it soon yielded three more rubies that were even bigger and of only slightly lower quality than the first. This time her brother, who ran the mine in her absence, decided to act legally, putting the stones up for auction at the annual Gems Emporium.

Coming from a lower-middle-class family, Hein had eloped with the only son of a wealthy family when she was in the seventh grade. After a few years of servitude in her parents-in-laws' home where she frequently quarreled with her sisters-in-laws, she finally erupted one day and caused a huge catfight. As a result, her parents-in-law, more in anger than generosity, gave their four children, including Hein's husband, equal shares of their fortune.

Hein said it was the best fight she had in her life, even though she was battered black and blue, for then she and her husband had the capital to set up their own business. She was the brains and the motivating force of their partnership and managed to increase profits a hundred times over within fifteen years. She said she wouldn't tell me all she had done for money but that she had done a great many things.

"I needed to make money, otherwise I would still be on a lower level than my in-laws," she shrugged. "I make it any way I can."

She was street-smart and once gave me advice I never forgot, which I think hinted at the success of her many deals. She told me not to expect from someone what he or she does not have in their character.

"Don't say 'she should be ashamed of herself' when you know that person has no shame," she told me. "It's a waste of your time and energy. A businessman who is extremely greedy will put financial profits above all else; he might cheat, lie, or even commit crimes, so don't ever wonder why he isn't ashamed to do any of these things. Someone who wants to be very famous will make that his priority. People who most value honor and integrity will never put money first and probably will never get rich, but will earn the respect of the community. People do things differently because they have different values and goals: know what they value, what their goals are, and you can work out what they will or will not do. Or, if you observe what they do, you can pretty much work out what their values are."

After my release in 1992, she fell ill and was sent out to the Guard Ward of the Yangon General Hospital, which offered a comfier bed. After a couple of general amnesties her sentence was reduced to ten years, the same as for the lifers who were once on death row for murder. Hein passed away about seven years after her release; she had several health problems even before she went to prison.

One person I liked a lot, and have not met again although I tried to, was Daw Hlaing Khin, who lives on forever in a corner of my mind. She was a vagrant, aged about sixty, who had been a prostitute when she was young.

She was rather skinny but traces of her beauty could be seen in her oval face with its high cheekbones, pointed chin, well-formed small nose, long black hair, and sparkling dark eyes under winged eyebrows. The straightness of her posture showed that she had once been a woman who wasn't to be overlooked. She was weather-beaten and tanned to a coppery tone when I met her but her ragged clothes were clean and neatly darned.

She had been in and out of jail many times, but I never saw her bow and scrape to anyone or even show any friendliness. The first time I noticed her was when she became an office helper, although I had heard of her before that.

My friends who crocheted would get skeins of white cotton which had to be rolled into balls before they could use them in their work. I had seen the cotton balls, which were unbelievably neat, as if rolled by a machine. I heard it was Daw Hlaing Khin's doing and had wanted to meet her so I could learn to do this, for my attitude toward any new task is that it might come in useful one day.

When I first saw her rolling a cotton ball near my window, she was sitting on an old reed mat on the bare ground. The skein was wrapped around her knees as she quickly and neatly rolled the cotton into a ball. I asked her politely how she did it, and she silently showed me. I could see she liked that I talked to her with respect, and from then on we were friends. But, suspecting she was proud, I didn't get chummy.

For a year her duty was to clean around the block and the office, so I saw her constantly. I thought she would hate to be under any sort of obligation so if I saw her standing in the yard, I would place a banana or a cookie on my windowsill, give her a nod, and sit down out of sight. She would then take it at her leisure. Slowly we became close and she eventually trusted me enough to tell me her story.

She had grown up an orphan, living with her aunt. At seventeen she had fallen in love with a neighbor, a handsome dancer in a traditional drama troupe. They eloped and she followed him on his tours. But he had other wives in other towns and used to pimp them, and her, to other men in his troupe and in the audience. She went back home, but she said she had begun to enjoy the excitement of meeting new men and she went professional. No pimps, she said, she preferred working alone. Her aunt threw her out so she rented a small house with several other working girls.

Some pimps tried to get her under their control but after she stabbed one in the thigh with a dagger she always carried, they left her alone. When she worked, she ate and dressed well. Once she was taken home by a foreigner, and she marveled at the exotic pleasure of soaking in a hot tub; he had insisted she bathe before they got down to business.

"I knew a few words of English," she said. "When he came cruising around our street I wasn't shy to go up and talk to him."

As she told me that story, describing the soft carpets and deep sofas in the foreigner's house, she laughed, her eyes sparkling like a girl's, and I could see how attractive she must have been.

Then, in her thirties, she met a gambling man, Ko Hlaing, who was also the head of a street gang who committed petty crimes and held illegal poker games. The two of them set up house in a small bamboo hut with a yard, and she stayed home to be a housewife. She had a hen coop with twenty chickens and a plot where she planted vegetables. He would go out in the morning and come home at night with fried noodles, half a roasted duck, or a salad made of crunchy pig's ears when he had won at cards or profited from a deal, which was often. She smiled with pride when she told me this and a look in her eyes revealed that she was completely lost in the past.

At night they would sit on the bamboo bench in front of the hut, she smoking small cheroots, he singing to her and playing a mandolin. They were together for thirteen years and she changed her name to Ma Hlaing Khin. One evening, coming home in the dark, her husband was bitten by a rabid dog. He died within a week, and she was back on the streets.

Her eyes dimmed as she told me this, but there were no tears. I had heard from others that she once drank a lot; very likely it was after she was widowed. I admired her aptitude for work, and her honesty, and her utter lack of hypocrisy. She became a prostitute not because she was lazy; she liked the work. She was never foul-mouthed or coy when she recounted her experiences, which she did in detail. Jailers would often raise their eyebrows at me when they saw us sitting together on a ragged mat, cozily conversing.

A few months before I was released the prison became overpopulated and a large group was sent to the rock quarries, including Daw Hlaing Khin. She went with her usual stoic expression on her face, head held high and refusing to look in my direction as I stared at her from my window, clutching at the bars. I never saw her again.

Another woman from the same profession was always neatly dressed, worked well, and took no nonsense from anyone. I was never close to her so I didn't learn her story but I often saw her competently doing her assigned work. When we had a lot of male prisoners around for our cellblock renovation, she didn't even glance at any of them.

I was surprised that someone like this woman, who could have done well in any job, had become a prostitute, but then, our conservative society at any level is unforgiving. Being a prostitute or even an unwed mother leaves such a stigma that it is no longer possible to return to "decent" society once coerced, forced, or tricked into the trade. Often enough, a girl became a sex worker when pimps went around the country pretending to be brokers who would get her a job as a maid in the city or, if she was pretty, pretended to fall in love and then elope with her. After a week of being held captive, raped, and beaten, the girl would be too ashamed to go home even if she could escape.

One elephantine but pretty girl, Jumbo, charmed us. She was about five feet seven inches tall, weighing about two hundred pounds, but she was very light on her feet. She had a cute face, curly light brown hair, and light brown eyes she said she inherited from her half-English grandmother. She loved to go to parties and had been caught at one where all the guys were smoking heroin while the girls danced. She was too deeply immersed in her disco moves to notice the other girls running out the back door when the police arrived, and she, the lone female among stoned men, was accused of being a druggie. She said proudly that it took four men to drag and push her into the Blue Maria and that one of them had begged her please not to get arrested again in his township, he didn't have the strength to incarcerate her again.

She still liked to dance, vocally providing her own music. John Travolta was her hero: she said she never recovered after seeing *Saturday Night Fever*. Aunty Hpaw loved to watch her dance and Jumbo didn't need much persuasion to entertain us. She wobbled all over as she enthusiastically threw her immense body and sweet soul into her moves and song. She was kind; she once wheedled (or stole) a packet of biscuits from someone and tossed it over a fence to me while I was out bathing, in the very early days when I wasn't getting any food parcels. The biscuits were crushed, but I have never tasted anything better. I licked up the crumbs, every bit, brushing aside the ants.

Another woman who was the same size as Jumbo was Hsin M'lite. She stole detachable parts from parked cars and would hide them between her enormous breasts; in those days when car parts were scarce, they fetched a good price. The policemen never dared search her body in public, but one day they brought along a policewoman in civvies. She had no hesitation about groping around Hsin M'lite's huge boobs where interesting things were tucked away, and at last Hsin M'lite landed in Insein for the first time.

She really hated policewomen: "They are women! They should be at home!" she would cry in outrage. She was freed after a few months but was soon back, bringing in a packet of menthol cigarettes for Nita, who had been kind to her. It was another policewoman who again had caught her, and Hsin M'lite was all the more enraged that women were taking up professions that were to her mind unladylike.

Love and marriage in vagrant society could be extremely casual. Once I overheard two Thirty D women sitting under my window, talking about the men in their lives. One was telling the other what a jerk her ex-husband was, and from what I could gather he was about the fourth ex.

"It was right there at the Bauk Htaw Station, that I divorced him," she said.

I was intrigued…divorce at a railway station?

"I took back the rubber flip-flops I had given him and gave him back the red shoulder bag he got me, and that was that: I told him he was no longer my spouse," she said. I related the story to my friends the next day and we, divorcées, lawyers, and contented wives, laughed at how smoothly she had managed the division of property.

Young Cho Pone, or "Sweet Pile," was a prostitute still young and romantic enough to fall in love with Sote Pwa, "Mussed Hair," a vagrant who was always in and out of prison and every day carried rice bins to us from the kitchens. He was also what we call *Lu Mite*, a bad boy, the gangster type who wouldn't hesitate to throw a brick at someone's head if enough money was offered to him. Somehow, while he was at the open gate, he and Cho Pone had caught sight of each other. After that Cho Pone waited every day at a place where she could see him and they would gaze mistily at each other.

I noticed them while I was out walking. I knew that Sote Pwa was a good chap at heart, and I felt so sorry for him that when he asked me to get the name of his lady love and find out when and from which police station she would be released, I did it. He was due to be released a week before she was, and he planned to wait at the police station to claim her.

Sote Pwa was very grateful for my help and offered to do me some serious favors. "Just tell me who you want to see with a broken head or crushed kneecap, Aunty, I'll do it for you, no charge…just tell me who and when and how many stitches you want in his head or which knee you want damaged," he often whispered to me at the gate. There is actually one man, the unfaithful husband of a very dear friend, whose knee-caps I would have loved to have Sote Pwa crush, but I had to consider how burdened my friend would be if she had to look after a cripple.

Cho Mar was a pretty, decent young woman with two daughters and a useless, jobless husband. She sold vegetables in the Ahlone Market, but looked so respectable and behaved so graciously that she would have been a delight in any social class. She was sentenced for six months because an illegal lottery ticket had been found on her.

An older, kindly man, not her lover but apparently someone who wooed her and looked after her, visited her and bought her a lot of food. It sounded as though he was deeply in love with her and we all hoped that the dimwit husband would be dumped as soon as possible. For a petty crime her spouse actually came inside, once, and managed to get over to the women's side by carrying the rice that the women had to pick over for grit and husks. We examined him critically, and all of us—jailers, guards, political prisoners, criminals, and vagrants—declared he wasn't good enough for her.

Ma Wai was a petty criminal, a woman over forty, but even with missing front teeth she was still so lovely that she could be mistaken for some-one ten years younger. Her husband was the legendary Yeikkha (Ogre), facing some forty charges of assault and battery, burglary, theft, you name it, he'd got it. She came in with her young son Belu (another word for ogre).

We had seen Yeikkha once or twice, when he came to our gate on errands sent by his jailer to ours, just so that he could see his wife and son. He worshipped his wife, who was ten years his senior. He was the one who had hidden a file in his shoe to cut away the bars in the window of the Blue Maria. His two companions escaped but while he was wriggling out as the last one, he was caught halfway through by a policewoman. Henceforth, inmates going out to face more charges had to go out barefoot, all of them cursing Yeikkha, whose name and deeds were known to all in Insein.

After we were released we still kept tabs on our erstwhile co-inmates and heard that Yeikkha was sent to a rock quarry. He escaped within a month and disappeared over the hills, meeting up somewhere with his wife and son, who were already released. I was told they crossed into Thailand some time later.

Nasty Daw Kyee Kan or Madame Crow, the Tan Zee and pickpocket, turned her livelihood into a family business, with her gang consisting of her offspring, their spouses, nephews, and nieces. I once asked her to teach me how to lift a wallet. But Madame Crow refused, saying only her family worked with her and she couldn't let outsiders in. My friends teased that if I were really serious I could always marry one of her brothers.

Madame Crow used to say in all seriousness that when she stole something she was only getting what the victim didn't deserve to possess. This statement, once made within the guard Ma Cho's hearing, earned her an extremely loud and colorful tongue-lashing.

Each August, when the *Taungpyone* Spirit Festival came around, the time when pickpockets make the most money, Madame Crow would be literally ill with longing to ply her trade there. Ma Nwei the guard said she saw her once at the train station near Taungpyone time, dressed in gaudy nylon, dripping with (possibly fake) gold jewelry, and felt so disgusted she wanted to puke.

(About six months after I was released I saw a small paragraph in the newspaper reporting that, having been let out the previous morning, Madame Crow was caught a couple of hours later cutting off a child's gold chain in Insein Market, which is about two blocks away from the prison. Back inside she went.)

Aye Mi San, another pickpocket, was once on a train where she sat next to a military officer. From his bag she lifted an army troop's pay packet. When she saw a notice in the paper that anyone who returned the important documents taken with the cash would be rewarded, she personally went to return the papers. The officer recognized her silver tooth, and in she came for three years. "Curse this stupid tooth! Curse stupid me!" she would cry when she told us this story. She was much nicer than Madame Crow and assured us that since she knew us now, she would never slit our bags if we should meet on buses or trains.

Tin Thein was the most irritating, cheating, lying criminal that I have ever met, as well as an accessory to first-degree murder, but none of us could help liking her. We knew she was cheating us and lying to us, and still we would laugh even when we were furious with her. She was an accessory to murder because, as she explained, she would willingly go to hell if the company was fun.

Her partners in crime were Yin Yin Myint, a quiet woman who was rather cold-blooded, and her husband, who later died in prison of cancer. They were all good friends from the same delta town. Yin Yin had a general store, and one crazy old woman often came to shop. One day she was so annoying that Yin's husband in a temper pushed her; the woman fell, hit her head on the edge of a step, and lost consciousness. They searched her and found a packet of diamonds among her rags, so the two of them bashed in her head.

Right after that Tin Thein sallied in for a visit. She tried to run when she saw what was going on, but Yin held her and begged her not to betray them but instead help them dispose of the body. They put the corpse in a large plastic bag and threw it into a stream, forgetting about the tide. Their victim floated inland and surfaced right next to the police station. As the news raged within their small town, Tin Thein confessed to her husband, who in terror told the police. She and her friends were sentenced to death, which was, much later, reduced to life imprisonment.

Before they were sent to Pathein Jail to be tried, Tin Thein and Yin Yin managed to break out of the local lockup and by nightfall they were well hidden in some bushes far in the woods. The police were searching in the vicinity, and one elderly chap called out: "You girls! Have a heart, I'm about to retire and if we can't find you I'll lose my pension." Tin Thein got up, shouting, "Yo! Over here!" and gave them all away.

Yin Yin nearly strangled her then and there and didn't seem to forgive her, for in Insein she kept apart from Tin Thein and everyone else. The others thought she was cruel and didn't approach her. Once when a group of vagrants were having a fight, Yin Yin, who was sitting nearby took up a small rock, cracked it against the head of one of the combatants, and calmly returned to her seat. The vagrants were so shocked that anyone could be that violent without being angry that they all hastened away, their fight forgotten.

Knowing I love cats, Tin Thein would often tell me about the mother cat and three kittens that lived in her cell in Pathein Jail. Very likely these beautiful, utterly clever felines that she described in detail existed only as a way to further Tin Thein's wily scheme to get sausages from me.

Once she scammed me for weeks, telling me that a cat had given birth to a litter of six in a corner of the hall farthest from my block. She promised to get me a kitten when it was old enough and I was so grateful that I gave her food every time she came to report on the health of the kittens. Earnestly she told me one kitten had died but the rest were doing fine, and described the colors of each, assuring me I could choose. I eagerly said I wanted the white one with ginger spots.

One day I mentioned it to Aunty Hpaw, who in bewilderment said there were no kittens anywhere. When I insisted that she make sure, she had to make a round of the halls, taking Pyone with her as a witness whom I would believe. When I found out the truth, it was such a clever scam that I was laughing even as I threatened to kill Tin Thein.

Tin Thein's exploits were numerous. She wasn't pretty but tall and gangly, with a long mannish face and a hangdog, mournful expression. Being a basketball player, she was muscular and looked somewhat masculine, but she wasn't gay. However, she would sometimes wear her longyi knotted in front like a man just to get admiring glances from the flirty Thirty Ds or get rations from those so inclined. There were rumors that her stash of diamonds was still safely hidden away, perhaps Tin Thein's ploy to get goodies out of anyone who believed she would share the loot once she got out.

She helped with the office work, doing errands within the women's compound, so she was often around our block. Sometimes the guards would ask her to sing, for she could do the old classics very well, songs that had been made famous on our traditional Zat theater stage. She would invent strangely odd lyrics if she didn't know the words. This was one thing that irritated me beyond reason, and while she was warbling away I would be gripping the bars of my cell and screaming at her, "Tin Thein, Shut up! These are not the proper lyrics," to which she paid not the slightest attention.

Her deadpan jokes left us gasping in laughter. When she smiled, which was seldom, it lit up her face and made her attractive. She somehow managed to look years younger than her age, in spite of the lack of any traces of femininity. She was perpetually on the lookout for scams so someone or other was always screaming at her, but nobody had the heart to get really angry.

No matter how much people shouted at her she was never resentful. Everybody liked her, although why none could say. She was never sweet or charming; in fact she spoke rather bluntly and usually had a gloomy expression on her face, but she was very popular. We used to say she must have been born with some sort of magic. It was she who had entertained us all with the dramatic performance that skyrocketed Shorty to fame in the role of the noisy infant.

About six months before I was released, Tin Thein and Yin Yin requested, and were granted, permission to be transferred to Pathein Jail, near their hometown on the western coast where their families could visit them more often. On the morning of their departure, few bid farewell to Yin; they all crowded around Tin Thein, giving her small gifts, many of them crying, stroking her hair, or petting her shoulder. Tin Thein looked gloomy, as usual, but she didn't cry. Yin looked as if she couldn't care less. I watched from my cell window and Pyone and Tin stared from the sidelines, all of us laughing at the fuss.

Another girl, Mi Lone or "Miss Round," had been adopted by a rich family when she was seven years old. After her mother died, her father had sold her when she was seven because he wanted to remarry. She grew up with the grandchildren of her adoptive family, learning to be polite and well mannered, and went to school for a few years. But of course she was a servant. She grew up to work as a maid but due to her childhood upbringing her manners were certainly better than the other criminals'.

At seventeen she was seduced by the night watchman next door. She used to sneak out late at night, taking her mosquito net, a mat, and pillow to sleep with him in the garden. After the affair had gone on for about six months, she had been conned into letting him into her house one midnight, believing he was going to help her pack and then elope with her. He tried to open the safe, but the household woke up and he brutally killed everyone in the family. He and his accomplice ran away with the money they found, which was around 30,000 kyat, probably no more than sixty U.S. dollars at that time. They were caught before seven the next morning, and sentenced to death. The watchman died in jail of illness before their sentences were reduced to life.

Mi Lone had been in jail for about three years. When rumors swept the prison about a general amnesty, she quaked with terror; she feared freedom as she had nowhere to go. She knew no one would dare take her in and she would probably become a vagrant or a prostitute. Freedom for her would be worse than prison.

Htay Htay was in jail for supposedly killing a thirteen-year-old girl when she was sixteen. Her trial took over two years, so she was of age when she was finally sentenced to death, a fate that was later changed to life imprisonment. She and the younger girl had been great friends and inseparable companions in a small up-country village.

Htay Htay's brother-in-law had first raped her when she was fourteen, and by the time she was sixteen it was very probable that it had turned into a long-standing affair. The younger girl had caught the two of them together one afternoon, and the brother-in-law killed the child for fear that she would tell his wife, who held the purse strings. He also took the girl's gold earrings and asked Htay Htay to keep them for him. Then, he persuaded her to confess to the murder, to say that she did it for the earrings. He convinced her that women were never sent to prison or punished for any crimes.

Htay Htay, who left school in the second grade to help her farmer parents, believed him and confessed. Her sister, still unaware of the truth, came to visit about once a year; she lived far in the north and couldn't afford to come more often. Htay Htay said that she would be satisfied if her brother-in-law came just once, to beg her pardon for lying to her. He never did.

They and other poor inmates did odd jobs for the more affluent prisoners, such as laundry and washing up after meals, receiving food and clothing in return. When people left prison, they usually left behind their clothes and other belongings for Htay Htay and her colleagues.

Another pair, two sisters named Kyi and Bi, whose younger brother was in the men's section, came from a conservative family. Kyi and her husband and their small daughter, the husband's widowed sister and her young daughter, plus Kyi's three younger siblings all lived in one small flat. The sister-in-law's child was mentally handicapped and often uncontrollable, making life difficult for the women cooped up in the house. Also, the widow liked to complain a lot to her brother so that Kyi and her sisters were frequently and unfairly punished, which made the widow crow with glee.

Frustration and rage exploded one day when the husband was away: Kyi used a stone mortar used for pounding chilies to batter her sister-in-law and her child to death. Her sister Bi and her young brother helped her cut up the bodies, packing them into plastic bags and then inside cardboard boxes. The youngest sister, who was out at the time and knew nothing, was told to dump them somewhere. She carried the boxes away on her bicycle and left them near a market. The bodies were found and all four arrested, for the clue was the husband who had reported his sister's disappearance with her child to the police. The youngest girl received a six-year sentence, and the three others were sentenced to death, later commuted to life.

Kyi's husband came to see her before they were sentenced and had said to her during one visit: "Why didn't you tell me? I wouldn't have reported her missing." She never saw him again after her sentencing; he took their daughter and went to live abroad.

(No woman was ever executed in prison. As far as I know, only five men have been hanged since Myanmar became independent in 1948, all for political offenses. They were Galon U Saw, who assassinated our national hero, General Aung San; Captain Ohn Kyaw Myint, who planned to assassinate U Ne Win; Ko Tin Mg Oo, a Communist student leader in the 1975 Hmaing Centenary riots; and two Karen National Union officers.)

There was one gentle, beautiful woman whose name I didn't know, who had accidentally and fatally stabbed her husband while they were alone and teasing each other in the kitchen as she was cutting vegetables. She was sentenced to seven years for involuntary manslaughter. Later we learned that he had been cheating on her for six months before he was killed, at which point she became a hero to every woman, prisoner and guard. She was much liked as she was decent, kind to others, and obviously well bred.

Once a transvestite who looked utterly feminine was sent to the women's side by mistake, since intensive body searches for women weren't part of the registration process; they just patted you down for anything hidden.

She/he was there for a month before someone noticed the out-of-place thing he had while he was at the outside loo. When it was reported with much alarm, the jailer marched her charge straight to the Main Jail, without checking to see if "it" was true. The guard who was taken along told me later that the female and male jailers spent fifteen minutes forcing each other to check: "You go first," "No, you do it."

Nobody was willing to risk touching private parts that weren't the same as their own. Finally it was verified. A male convict helping around the office was ordered to do it, and the transvestite was sent to a special place where those of similar orientation were kept separate from the straight male convicts.

The drug dealers in jail tried their best to continue with their business even from prison, and many clampdowns on what was permitted in food parcels occurred because of them. Once we couldn't get sugar or milk powder for several months because a dealer from the men's side tried to smuggle heroin in them and was caught. Later on sugar and milk powder were only available when sold from the prison shop in sealed bags.

Dealers were thoroughly hated by everyone in prison and nobody would speak to them. The dirtiest, poorest prostitutes would say that they might sell their bodies but sure as hell they would never kill other people's children by selling drugs.

Babies and toddlers lived in jail, some clean, some grubby, but all looked after one way or the other. Some mothers were lazy and left their children to their own devices, whereupon they were fed, bathed, and cared for by others. When a mother was poor or ill, other equally poor women helped her, washing her clothes, nursing her baby, and working to get her nicer food.

When there was no one at home to look after them on the outside, children up to seven years of age were allowed to accompany their parents to jail, sons with their fathers, daughters with their mothers. If a woman convict had a son, he was allowed to stay with her, and fathers could keep their sons. However, if a man came in with a daughter, she was placed in the women's compound where the inmates looked after her and pampered her. The jailers usually managed to give the father a job that let him to come up to the gate of the women's section, where he could look at his child and hold her for a few minutes.

There was one case of a convict bringing in a daughter of about three who was sent to our section to stay for the duration of his six-month sentence.

Every day the little girl was freshly bathed, covered with thanakha paste, and dressed in donated frocks to greet her daddy when he came with the rice bins. When he was released her foster mothers were happy to see her go free but cried their eyes out at the same time. The father thanked the women repeatedly, tears streaming down his face as he held his daughter tightly. He said he was going to take her away from the city and go back to his village where life was simpler.

Clothes for the prison children were often donated by wealthier inmates whose children had outgrown them. Some prisoners asked their families to buy them children's clothes, including Pyone, Tin, and Mar, who contributed a great deal toward outfitting the prison's child population. Their husbands were astounded, asking them, "Baby clothes? What do you want baby clothes for?" but were told it was none of their business.

"We say that outside, too, all the time, so why stop now?" they said when I asked them to have mercy on the poor guys.

Mean Miss Chili Pepper loved babies. She would bathe, feed, and look after the prettier ones when their mothers were busy. Even to the not-so-pretty ones she was kind, which coming from her was totally amazing, but then she had two young sons of her own.

There was one cute little baby girl, so pretty with curling lashes and dimples, who came in when her mother was convicted for drug dealing. Her name was Cherry Pan or "Cherry Flower," but she was usually called Pan Pan. She was everybody's pet, especially Chili Pepper's, who wanted to adopt her and marry her off to her own son when the baby grew up.

Pan Pan's lazy mother seldom had to do anything for Little Miss Flower. I heard that later someone else's family took her in. Pan Pan was always well dressed, pretty, and pampered, but unspoiled for all that.

Ma Khaing, a prostitute, so decent-looking you would think she was a schoolteacher, had a baby while she was in jail. During her pregnancy she talked constantly about giving it away; she didn't even want to see "it," and there were a lot of women willing to adopt the child. But once the boy was born she wouldn't even let anyone else hold him. The beautiful baby boy left with her when she was released about a month after his birth.

One pregnant vagrant girl was so modest that she didn't report when her birth pains started. She began to go into labor on Aunty Hpaw's day off and feared that a male doctor would come to check on her and see her "down there," as she later explained to the jailer who was rendered speechless by this statement. The mother-to-be gathered a few of her friends and with their help successfully gave birth to a baby boy in a corner of the outside loos. That was in the days before we had a lady doctor and nurses.

Prison children received vitamins, nutritious rations, and sometimes, milk powder. All day long they wandered around in a large group without any need for supervision, since there was no traffic to worry about. They played at bringing in the rice bins, sitting to be counted, lining up to get rice—all the things they saw daily.

They knew airplanes and birds but they didn't know cars or trains or ships, cats or dogs. Once, seeing a huge rat run through a drain they cried out in unison, "Doggy! Doggy!" while running after it, hoping, they told their mothers later, to make it a pet.

They saw male jailers, the male doctor, or the electricians, all of whom wore uniforms, but they had no conception of what a man was when they saw one in civvies. One evening Hein was outside during her exercise period and a group of toddlers was playing nearby. A man was up on a pole fixing a wire, but he wasn't wearing a uniform since it was an emergency and he had been called from his home.

"What is that?" the kids asked her, pointing up at him.

"That's a man," she replied

"What's a man?" they asked.

"Uh, a man is…" Hein was stumped, as she told me later. "He's like your daddy! That's it, your daddy is also a man!" she told them finally.

Then all the toddlers ran to the foot of the ladder screaming, "Daddy! Daddy!" as they looked up at the poor man, nearly making him tumble off his ladder in shock.

10. PEST CONTROL

The rats running around the planted vegetables were so fat and huge that it was no wonder the toddlers thought they were dogs. Fortunately they didn't enter our cellblock; we had more than enough pests already and struggled to control their population, especially the bedbugs.

I had my plastic sheet as protection against bedbugs, but in the early days when others had not yet managed to get sheets sent in by families, bedbugs were more than pests. They were horrifying and disgusting. Their bites left clusters of itchy red bumps that gave us goose pimples of revulsion, even if we only had to look at them. Living deep within the mats or the cracks in the wooden platforms, or the planks of the upper halls, at night they marched out in armies to devour us. Mar Mar, the constant supporter of matrimonial bliss, used up her time plucking bedbugs from the cracks in her wooden sleeping platform and drowning them in a bowl of water.

We knew there was a very effective bedbug killer sold under the brand Polo with a distinct foul smell, but it was poisonous. We had to beg the jailers many times to let us have some because they were afraid we would use it to commit suicide. Finally our families were allowed to send in a few bottles, and after several dousing sessions with a rag soaked in a diluted solution of this chemical, we had no more bedbugs. It was so poisonous that when we used it, we had to cover our hands with plastic bags.

The other pests, which didn't bother me at all, were the mice living between the two layers of wooden planks that separated our cells. I rather liked them, although none of my cellblock mates shared that feeling.

Although the others couldn't abide them, the mice weren't dirty rats but rotund, black creatures with shiny, sleek fur. Their ears were large pink coins, translucent against the light. Their bare long tails were brownish pink. They had clean, tiny pink paws and they stole any food that wasn't covered up or tied up in bags. The prison rats, in contrast, had dirty, scraggly fur; we would often see about six of them running in a line, with the tail of the one in front clamped in the teeth of the one behind.

I must admit that I was entirely responsible, if not intentionally so, for the rise in the mouse population. I pushed food into the cracks in the wooden planks of the walls but dared not tell anyone I was feeding the mice, as everyone else was screaming about them. The most they got from any other prisoner was when a few of my cellblock mates piled a bit of rice in one corner to keep them away from other food.

It wasn't that the mice were really pets to me, but in memory of another member of their vast family I was kind to them.

Before my involvement in politics, there was one mouse of the same breed that had the run of my small house. She was a cute roly-poly little black thing I named Wilhelmina. She would scoot around the house, turning corners at such a fast clip she flew off the floor, very much the way that action heroes in the movies drive around street corners. Unfortunately, she gave birth to seven babies, after making a nest among the wires of my hi-fi system which she first chewed up...and which took six months to be repaired as during the bleak Socialist era there were no spare parts available.

A few of her children drowned in the can of turpentine in which I washed my paintbrushes. They also left tiny paw prints in all colors on my canvases, no doubt improving my artwork. I was quite happy to see

Wilhelmina's cousins with me now in jail—she had quite an extended family.

Some of them would run along the upper ledge of the wall in my cell at a moment when I sneezed. They would jump in terror at the sound and then drop down to the floor, sometimes crashing onto the cover of my loo basin. After the third time this happened, I was careful to check if any mice were endangered when I felt a sneeze coming on.

At other times they would peer into the next cell through cracks in the wall, probably checking for food, and their long tails would dangle out on my side of the wall.

I would gently take the tip of the tail in my fingers and swing it as I would a bell rope. It was so funny to see them turn around slowly, with a horrified look on their faces—"What was that?"—then scamper off as fast as their tiny pink paws could run. My friends thought this was disgusting. I was actually touching mice! I was touching their tails! But I was grateful that the mice gave me something to laugh about.

When I was caught red-handed by Aunty San, who peered into my front window just as I was poking food through the walls, she and the others all to a woman denounced me soundly. They said it was my full responsibility that the mouse population seemed to have expanded five times over, and I confessed with due humility.

It was true that the mouse birth rate got out of hand, but it also meant that to get rid of the mice, our wooden walls had to be replaced with brick. The others refused to thank me when I declared they should, as I was the one who increased the mouse population enough to have the renovation done. Thus I was indirectly responsible for our few days of freedom, as we had to stay outdoors while male prisoners worked inside.

Some months before the renovation, we thought of getting cats for mouse control and once by straight-out thievery and once through kindness, we did manage to have a couple of cats at different times. I felt sorry for the mice but I desperately longed for a cat.

The kitchens had many cats to keep down the mice, and so did the men's section. However, the men were possessive of their pets and wouldn't spare us any, no matter how many times we pleaded with the rice-bin-carrier convicts. We even enlisted the male guards, through messages passed by their wives, our guards, who spoke on our behalf. Nothing worked.

At last, Hein, the wealthy inmate in the cellblock, bribed a male prisoner with a very expensive bundle of food to get us a cat, by any means. The next day when he brought the rice bins he also brought us a kitten wrapped in a rag, a skinny black female we named Missy Black.

Our "dealer" was very nervous, saying he had to steal her from the kitchens. She was one of rather a large litter so he hoped she wouldn't be missed. We thought it quite fair to have the kitten even though she was stolen goods, because the kitchen staff of convicts already had so many cats.

This tiny black thing was an immediate success, going to work at once and catching three mice within the first five minutes. We all applauded her skills even as I felt sorry for the poor mice, which she didn't eat but decapitated and laid out in a row. She climbed busily in and out of each cell through a small hole in the window screen.

Disaster struck in three days. One fat, important-looking, but grimy prisoner came to our gate attended by a male guard. Later we found out he was the chief cook and a lifer. The two of them looked sternly at Aunty Hpaw, who had opened the door.

"You have our cat," the cook announced, staring disdainfully over Aunty Hpaw's head. "It was stolen."

Aunty Hpaw turned pale: she knew all about our theft. Lips quivering in apprehension, she turned to glance imploringly at some of us, who were out for exercise. We stood rooted, fear in our hearts.

Daw Aye Aye Than, who was sitting at her desk, jumped to her feet to defend us. "No, we don't," she declared. "What cat are you talking about?"

"That one." The male guard pointed at Missy Black, who just that minute strolled out from the front door of the cellblock.

They took her away in triumph, leaving a number of cat lovers with broken hearts and the mice haters in despair.

We were so desolate about our loss that finally the nice Karen guard, Ah Moe, smuggled in another. We named her Missy Meow; she was sleek, black and white, and on the skinny side. We soon learned she had a mind of her own. She was a good mouser, and we settled down to enjoying our time with her. Within several days the mice had moved out, but by then the plans for replacing the wooden walls were already in place. Missy Meow remained queen of the block, utterly spoilt and pampered. Her intelligence is still talked about by the cat lovers who had lived under her rule.

A pair of political prisoner sisters who were devoted to her asked their family to send in imported packets of processed milk, a rare and expensive commodity at the time, just for Missy. The first time she was given this milk she memorized where it came from, and ever afterward when she spotted the packs of milk in anyone's parcel, she would pat it with her paw. If this polite gesture was ignored, she would tear the bag open with her claws.

Our friend Ma Ohn from Central Myanmar with five kitties at home was more a devout Buddhist than a cat lover. Every morning she prayed in front of an offering of a small plate of food as a gesture of gratitude to the Buddha, the same way she would at her shrine at home. Once while she was praying, Missy strolled in and tried to snatch the small piece of fried fish on the offering plate. Ma Ohn swatted lightly at Missy's head and continued praying. From that time on, Missy refused to eat fried fish from Ma Ohn's hand, however many times it was offered to her, although she ate it from others. Apologies weren't accepted.

When my room had baby sparrows flopping about and Missy one day tried to climb through the hand-hole in the window screen, I shooed her away and then tied strings across the opening so that she couldn't get in. Long after that batch of birds was gone and the strings removed, she wouldn't come into my room even if dragged or pulled: she resisted with all her might, clawing and fighting. But she was gracious enough to allow me to carry her on my shoulders as I walked up and down during my exercise time. She loved to perch there as we walked and would be passed from one person to the next in turn. Her tail swishing gently, she would look over our shoulders to apparently enjoy the view from this elevated height.

One day I started singing softly to her as she rested against my shoulder and she seemed to enjoy it; her tail swung in wide arcs. The sisters who had pampered her with imported milk looked out their window at us and groaned, "Oh no, Aunty Lay, now you've done it, she's going to expect us to sing too and you know we can't carry a tune. She won't like that!"

After they were released, the sisters managed to bring Missy Meow out of jail to live with them at home; it was a successful prison break.

11. LAST DAYS

One day during the last week of February of 1992, I was told to be dressed and ready. I thought I would be taken to another interrogation. After my first six months in prison they had tapered off, but I was still questioned about once every four or five months. The hood placed on my head for these outings was kept in the office cupboard, and I saw to it that it was washed frequently, so that it wouldn't smell musty.

This time, wearing no hood, I was led out to a small closed van. Inside, with joy and apprehension, I met four of my friends from the men's side: Ko Maw, my old colleague; the artist Ko Myoe; the student Moe Myat; and Kyaw Thura, the youngest and the tallest of the student bodyguards. We sat close together, clutching hands and grinning at each other. We were driven out to a low brick building that I knew was the martial court, just outside of the main entrance. We were put in separate rooms, left to sit and wonder for an hour, then were driven back without any explanation.

A week later we were taken out again. This time Kyaw Thura, who sat next to me, whispered into my ear that most of the others had been released. I felt a sudden surge of joy, tinged with a certainty, which I could see in their eyes as well, that we wouldn't be going home. Just as we got down from the van, I saw a large crowd some yards away looking over at us. I squinted in the harsh sunlight and when someone waved both arms and began jumping up and down, I recognized Tiger.

He was one of a large group of students who helped Ma Suu; he had loaned his car and himself as driver, in Yangon and on our overnight trips. He was a very good-natured chap, and on long drives to keep him from nodding off I had to keep feeding him sour pickled fruit. One evening, before embarking on a trip that would take more than half a night's driving, I made my special black coffee and told Tiger to drink it all. He took a gulp and promptly threw up. Watching with folded arms I made him drink some more. Later he came to prefer this coffee, as I forced it on him so many times to keep him awake.

I later found out that he had been coming to watch for us at this court every day after his release, since no one was told when we would be tried at this military tribunal. He just wanted to say hello, and we were happy to see him grinning widely and jumping like a dancing bear, thick arms waving in the air. He was very strong; two or three times on our campaign trips when I wasn't fast enough to make it onto a moving train, truck, or jeep, he grabbed me by the waist and simply pushed me headfirst like a log of wood through the nearest window or threw me on the vehicle like a bag of garbage.

This time we were led into the court, with three judges in uniform sitting on a stage, one from the navy, one from the air force, one infantry. The boys and I sat in a row, staring around inquisitively. We smiled at each other and held hands. The charges were made, which were only too true, so we had to admit that we had indeed committed them. If there had been charges of something we had not done at all, we were prepared to argue our innocence of them for however long it took.

To our utter astonishment and his joy, the youngest but the tallest, Kyaw Thura, was charged with being our leader. Our leader? We older ones glared at the judges upon this insult and stared in horror at each other and at "our leader." He was very pleased to have this honor and grinned down at us from his six-foot-four-inch height.

We all knew it was a deliberate dig at us older ones by the Military

Intelligence. In spite of our positions on opposite sides, our clashes were sometimes a game designed to make the other side squirm. When they would follow us around and take pictures, we would pose and then demand copies of the photos. When on our travels, we used to ask them if we could hitch a ride in their cars or on their motorbikes. They were less mischievous than we were and their official positions prohibited them from behaving as we did. But now, they were getting back at us by making this kid our leader.

Kyaw Thura and the other three were sentenced to eight years each, and my heart felt torn to hear the words. How would his mother, a sweet, good-hearted lady, feel when she heard this? He didn't seem disturbed, and the others' cocky expressions remained intact.

Then it was my turn: ten years. The guys looked at me, visibly upset. By now I was very piqued that this kid should have been named my leader and my sentence only added insult to that injury.

During the sentencing, one judge had remarked that we were political prisoners. This to my knowledge was the first ever official reference made to any of us prisoners being political, and I thought I should emphasize it. I requested in a firm tone that since we were considered political prisoners we should be allowed mosquito nets and reading material. I knew very well none would be forthcoming; it was merely to repeat legally and formally what he had called us. I wasn't about to miss that chance.

There was some hurried chatter about how things were with the other boys (they were freed! Wonderful news! But the older guys such as U Win Htein were still there...), and then we were sent back to our cells. My friends in the cellblock were anxiously waiting for me, and I first felt a pang for the look on their faces, full of sympathy and pain. I remembered that many others were under sentences more than double my own and yet they were sad for me.

Immediately Ma Aye Mon said that I must write an appeal. I refused since I knew it would be useless but she insisted it was just part of the normal procedure. So I wrote a short but polite note, something like "All Right, Release Me Already." Ma Aye Mon said dryly that if she passed that on I would probably get a few additional years, and that she would rewrite it for me. I told her not to make it a begging or fawning letter and she agreed. The finished letter was to the point and acceptable, so I signed it.

After I was sentenced, I could have visitors.

The first to come was the friend who lived in the same building where I had resided, the one who had been sending me food parcels. She wasn't allowed this first time to bring a lot of food, but she brought more than enough. I had to talk to her with a double screen between us with three officers present, plus my jailer, Daw Aye Aye Than. Two of them took notes on what we said. My mother, who lived at another address, needed to get permission to see me, but that could be easily arranged.

When I came back, Tiny, as usual up to mischief, sent word to my friends in the hall that it was my ex-husband who came, that he had brought nothing, and I was crying. She did this because, as she explained, "Your friends will send over food, just wait and see, and we'll split the loot fifty-fifty."

As I never cry unless at bad novels or bad movies, I was game to see who would believe this. Sure enough my friends sent me bags of food through the guards and Tiny got her half. It was a good joke that everyone enjoyed, even the kindhearted donors. In their worry for me, they had forgotten the cardinal rule—never trust Tiny.

Tuesday came, and I asked the senior jailers on their weekly rounds to allow my mother to visit me. By chance, about six sparrows were loose and hopping about on the floor and the male jailers became quite captivated, excitedly talking to each other about the birds. None of them heard the request I made about my mother. As they left my door they were still talking about the sparrows. "So sweet! How tame!" Before going after them, Daw Aye Aye Than rolled her eyes, gave me an amused look, and said that she would submit my request in person later. It was granted.

Mother came to see me on the next visitors' day, and as soon as she saw me in prison whites she burst into tears...I had never seen her cry like this before or even in a more restrained manner. Mum simply never cried.

I said to her, "Mum, hey, look at me, I'm fine. Mum, don't cry."

Seeing that I was made up to the nines, if not dressed in the same way she was used to seeing me in the past, she stopped crying immediately and said, "You've always been tough your whole life like a *Pyit Taing Taung* (knockabout toy that stays upright) so I wasn't too worried about you." So true.

After hearing of my sentencing, my cousin who looked after my dog Bibi sat her down for a serious talk, telling her that it might be a long time before she saw me again since I had been sentenced to ten years. Bibi looked up into her face and listened very intently, my cousin told me later, her usual happy tail absolutely still. Two days afterward Bibi was found dead, apparently from a heart attack.

Days passed as usual; the weather was hot, the air humid.

The Water Festival and Myanmar New Year of mid-April came and went; we had a good time as usual. I mixed lemon squash that my friend Kelvin had sent in a large plastic bowl and gave a straw each to my friends. A competition, I announced: we would see who could drink for the longest time without raising her head when I said go.

Of course Hein won hands down (she told us not to underestimate the motivation of greed in any situation), Ma Hlaing came a close second, Nita choked, Ma Ohn couldn't even get her head in among the shoving throng, and Aunty San was still wondering what to do when the lemonade was all gone. We wisely didn't invite Tiny to participate.

One night in late April I dreamed that I was being sent to Pathein Prison, and furthermore without guards: I was going to have to find my own way to the prison after my boat docked there in the morning.

In my dream, Pathein, a delta town, was crowded; in the downtown area, steps by the side of the road led to streets on a higher level. I kept getting lost, and I repeatedly asked my way of people who kept pointing upward. I climbed the stairs but could see no sign of any jail. I was still trying to get back into prison, feeling very anxious, when I woke up. It was a strangely clear dream, and as I sat in my cell after taking my bath, I told Nita about it, laughing at how I was trying so hard to find my way back to jail.

I was thanakha'ed for the day, my red lipstick in place. As I talked to her I set out scraps of fabric to make some more stuffed turtles. I was on a roll. I'd been making turtles for over a month by then.

The dream turned out to be not so strange after all, for at about 10 a.m., Nita and I were told to pack. We were free.

It was April 26, 1992, one month and three days after I had been sentenced to ten years.

The suspended sentence still remains intact, for as Daw Myint Myint Khin, my lawyer, explained: "You haven't used it up yet."

We were taken to the office at the Main Gate and were given back the cash and jewelry we had brought in with us; I had no jewelry with me, only some cash and coins, with every note and coin accounted for.

After signing for this we were taken into a hall. I saw many NLD elders there; I think there were about twenty of us, with Nita and I the only women. One army officer gave a speech, and all I remember was that he said we were being released under Special Order 11/92 and that suspended sentences meant that if we were arrested again, these years would be added to the new sentence. During the speech I steadily looked at the photo of our hero Bo Gyoke Aung San hanging on the wall in front of us.

Then we were allowed to see our families while cameras of the state media flashed. Mother was waiting for me and gave her driver directions to a friend's house. I would stay there for a few months before buying a flat after I sold a tiny plot of land in a very expensive area. Mother lived too far out of town and I didn't want to be too much out of the way.

I only went out to see the families of those still left inside; I didn't go out again. Yangon after three years behind walls was too crowded and too noisy. Besides, many of my friends were still in prison and I felt miserable about that. I had no desire at all to eat any of the food I had longed for; I stayed home, reading anything I could get my hands on.

Fortunately my friends, both men and women, including the MPs, were all released over the next three months, apart from the BCP-connected inmates. I think about a hundred of us came out under Order 11/92. I felt somewhat happy after that, but still wished that Swe and Ma Sein Bin could be with us.

When we met or talked to friends, we would talk about the jokes we played on each other, the mischief we got up to just for the fun of it, the songs and stories we shared. Our families were relieved that we had not been sunk in despair and somewhat annoyed that we seemed to have had a lark. We were supposed to be miserable, we told our families, and we were damned if we'd oblige. But we continued talking so much about the fun we had that after three months everyone else got thoroughly fed up and refused to listen anymore.

We exchanged stories with our male colleagues; one of them had mixed red mud with water to create what looked exactly like the tea we get in our tea shops, strong and mixed with condensed milk. He had filled plastic bags with this concoction and sent it to friends in other cells on April Fool's Day. He was immensely satisfied that a few had actually gulped it down.

One evening in May, most of us released political prisoners of my generation who lived in Yangon had a reunion dinner at a Chinese restaurant with our families. Near closing time we decided to continue the evening at someone's house. It wasn't far from the restaurant and a number of us decided to walk.

It began to drizzle and my friends' wives urged us to get into their cars. We declined, saying nothing could be better than walking at night, in the rain, because we had been locked in every single night for the past three years. Those of us who had climbed into cars got right out again and we walked, in rows five or six abreast, on the empty streets.

As we strode with almost matching steps, I thought this was one of the best tastes of freedom, these fine drops of rain falling on our faces in the darkness of a late, late night.

YOU CAN SKIP THIS

Friends who were aware I was planning on writing this book suggested that the reader might like to know something about me. I am not enthusiastic about it but here it is, and there is no loss to anyone if the reader skips it altogether.

My paternal great-grandfather, U Paw Shan, was a Burmese (the majority race) and a landowner of Sagaing whose twenty or so concubines spent all his wealth. The only son by his legal wife, my grandfather U San Mya, went to college in India, got a BABL degree, and became a judge who served under the colonial British. My father, John Tin Tut, went to St. Peter's Boarding School in Mandalay and St. Paul's in Yangon while his parents were posted all over the country.

My maternal great-great-grandfather, U Pein, was a minister at the court of King Thibaw, our last monarch. His daughter and my great-grandmother, Khin Khin Lay, was a handmaiden to the Chief Queen Supaya Lat. She married Maung Maung Kywe, a Royal Reader. They too were Burmese. When the British colonized our country in 1885 and exiled the king and his family to India, Maung Maung Kywe and Khin Khin Lay left the palace compound to live in Mandalay.

Their second daughter, Khin Khin Toh, married Maung San, the son of a Chinese jade merchant and a Thai lady who was from a family of Ramayana performers brought back from a war with Ayutthaya in 1767.

Their second child was my mother, Khin Khin May (aka May Tin Tut after she married my father), who attended the American Baptist Mission School in Mandalay.

My parents met at Rangoon University in the 1930s. Father's family served under the British so Mother's side considered them traitors; hers served the king so the other side thought they were outdated. Ignoring the attitudes of both sides, my parents settled in Yangon and had two children, my brother and me.

After Myanmar became independent in 1948, my mother, Daw May Tin Tut, became a faculty member of Rangoon University's Philosophy Department, and my father, U Tin Tut, worked for the U.S. Embassy as a political advisor.

My brother and I attended the Methodist English High School of Yangon. Among our schoolmates were, as I mentioned earlier, Ma Suu, but also children of Premier U Nu and Socialist dictator General Ne Win; descendants of the various branches of the Burmese royal family and those who served them; scions of Shan rulers, including the two daughters of Sao Kya Seng (whose wife, Inge Sargent, wrote *Twilight over Burma*), and the children of Sao Shwe Thaike and Mahn Win Maung, two of the three presidents of the post-independence democratic era. (Sao Shwe Thaike's son, our schoolmate Myee Myee, was killed on the night of March 2, 1962, during the coup d'état by General Ne Win.) There were children of political figures such as Bo Letyar, Bo Setkyar, and U Kyaw Nyein. Among our alumni are movie stars, pop singers, respected scholars, successful professionals, famous artists, high government officials or military personnel, diplomats, exiled activists…but no Communists. We have annual reunions in Yangon and our biannual international reunions are held in places like London, Bangkok, Los Angeles, or Las Vegas.

After high school I went to the Institute of Economics and not art school as I preferred because Mother insisted I get a degree. However,

I took evening classes at the State School of Fine Arts and loved every minute. My first group exhibition, which was my debut as a professional painter, was in 1967. So far I have had seven solo shows apart from participation in many group exhibitions, including two duo shows with Khin, who has been my best friend since we were ten.

After graduating with a bachelor's degree in commerce, I took German and then French diploma courses at the Institute of Foreign Languages. By then I was married to a Myanmar diplomat. We had no children and divorced amicably in 1986. Two years later the uprising of 1988 happened and in August of that year I became Ma Suu's personal assistant.

In early 1989 I told her that after the elections, scheduled for May of the following year, I would like to return to my profession in art; office work wasn't a long-term career choice for me. Ma Suu agreed. In July 1989 she was put under house arrest and I was sent to Insein Prison, from which I was released in April 1992 with a ten-year suspended sentence.

After Ma Suu was released from house arrest on July 10, 1995, I worked a few days for her while handing over my duties to someone else. Since my work in politics was to look after her needs, ever since I left my post as her assistant I have no longer been officially involved with Ma Suu or, through her, indirectly with the NLD. However, I keep up with my connections and interest in the political and economic situations of my country.

At present, I live in Yangon and devote my time to writing about Things Myanmar.

ABOUT THE AUTHOR

Ma Thanegi was born in Myanmar and educated at the Methodist English High School, the Yangon State School of Fine Arts, the Institute of Economics and the Institute of Foreign Languages, where she learned German and French. She is a painter who has exhibited with group shows since 1967 as well as in seven solo exhibitions. She is a contributing editor at *The Myanmar Times*, an English language weekly. She has written many articles and numerous books on Things Myanmar.

She lives in Yangon.

Her email is mathanegi.writer@gmail.com

ALSO BY MA THANEGI

*Defiled on the Ayeyarwaddy:
One Woman's Mid-Life Travel Adventures on Myanmar's Great River*
2010, ThingsAsian Press, 5 1/2 x 8 1/2
inches; paperback; 256 pages; color
images
ISBN-10: 1-934159-24-7
ISBN-13: 978-1-934159-24-8
$12.95

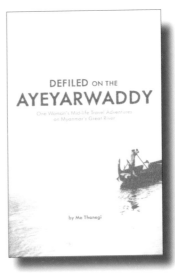

As she approaches her sixties, Ma
Thanegi decides to satisfy a lifelong
dream. Jumping on any boat that would
let her onboard, she begins a leisurely
exploration of Myanmar's thirteen
hundred-mile long Ayeyarwaddy River.
Always hungry—for food, conversation,
and a good story—Ma Thanegi clearly savors and vividly
describes every adventure she encounters, whether she is
traveling into the Cyclone Nargis-stricken delta region,
feeding a dragon, or careening down the rock-infested
white-water gorge of the Ayeyarwaddy's First Defile. You'll
love accompanying this opinionated and delightful lady
on an odyssey that takes her through much of Myanmar—
never without great passion for her country, a wicked sense
of humor, and her tube of red lipstick.

From *Defiled on the Ayeyarwaddy*
Chapter 1: Dancing at the Manau

My first steps toward a ride down the thirteen hundred-mile Ayeyar-waddy River began with a roll of drums, although not at all on my account. It was at a celebration on the northern tip of Myanmar and is-sued from great twenty-foot-long drums beaten by well-muscled Kachin men.

"There's going to be a major Kachin Manau festival in Myitkyina, right after Christmas," said Ko Sonny Nyein. A sculptor and painter, Ko Sonny and I go way back, at least twenty-five years, when we first met as members of the Peacock Gallery in Yangon.

Ko Sonny and his wife Amy are quiet and conservative by nature and hover over me like guardian angels—Ko Sonny rather like a tubby winged one. Both of them are constantly appalled at the risks I take in traveling alone, although it is very safe to travel in my country, and as a woman in my very mature years, I face no flirty harassment.

I knew that it was with grave misgivings that he invited me on this trip. Myitkyina is a civilized town in the Kachin State, full of well-behaved Christians and Buddhists, but Ko Sonny worries needlessly and all the time. Besides, he knows I like to veer off into unplanned routes.

The Kachin is one of the largest ethnic groups in Myanmar, living in the northeast of the country among wide plains and mountains. Their land has jungles, ice-capped mountains, and rivers. It produces gold and the best jade in the world, the Imperial Jade of the translucent grass-green so prized by the Chinese as a stone of honor and good fortune. This jade is found in astonishing abundance; a seventy-foot-long massive boulder was found in 2001 on New Year's Day, forty feet underground. The min-ing company willingly handed it over to our country, saying something of this immensity should be handled by the national government.

Defiled on the Ayeyarwaddy

I could not imagine what I would have carved out of this, given a chance—six billion pairs of earrings, maybe—but more likely the very first item that will be carved from it will be a Buddha image, bet you anything. As a Buddhist country of deep beliefs, Myanmar has tens of thousands of pagodas of every size dotted all over the country and uncountable Buddha images, with new ones being made every hour.

The people of the Kachin State also make woven cloth in red and black patterns, cane ware, and, most important to me, great food. Their food may be an acquired taste for Westerners, but for Myanmar palates, authentic Kachin noodles with pickled bamboo shoots or rice-tofu salad swimming in gravy or minced pork wrapped in banana leaves are gourmet meals which are not available in Yangon. They also have the sweetest pineapples and a nut called nga pauk which is creamier than the best pistachios. A famous French restaurant in Yangon, Le Planteur, drizzles nga pauk oil in a circle around their filet mignon.

Another fruit that I have not found anywhere else but in the Kachin State is the star apple, and people from other countries whom I have asked do not know it at all. It has a shiny, thin rind which is either maroon or green in color, and is the size of an apple. The inside is full of white, creamy, custardy flesh, with five small black seeds, and is said to be full of nicotine. I could eat twenty at a sitting, halving them with the penknife that I always carry with me and scooping out the flesh with a spoon which—needless to say—I always have on hand as well. Since I gave up smoking years ago, I feel I can afford to indulge in nicotine in this other form.

The Manau is a Kachin celebration for a good harvest or for the New Year, a public affair where clans gather. This one, to be held in Myitkyina over eight days starting on December 26, 2001, was on a scale that had not been seen for a hundred years. It would be a gathering of the eleven Kachin ethnic groups, the Jinghpaw, Trone, Dalaung, Guari, Hkahku, Duleng, Maru, Rawang, Lashi, Arsi and Lisu, and their subtribes, with other neighboring groups such as the Shan, Pa-O, and Palaung invited as well. Even tribes from across the border in China would attend, and the news went to Kachin ethnic groups living in the United States, Canada, and other countries overseas.

This festival was announced in September, and we were determined to go, with plans to leave on December 23. Most annoyingly, just one airline flew to this corner of the country so it would be hard to get flights that would bring us home; we could only book one-way flights from Yangon. Lucky me—I was not planning on flying back if I could help it.

By the morning of the twenty-fifth I was still sitting in my flat, fuming as I waited for tickets. It seemed that even one-way tickets from Yangon were difficult to obtain. All the flights were full and, since seats could not be booked until one day beforehand, and since priority was given to VIPs or foreigners who needed to connect with outgoing planes, locals were usually held over in a long waiting line. All this fuss for a few days' stay in Myitkyina, I thought, growing desperate.

Confident that I would leave on the twenty-third, I had airily refused all Christmas invitations, so I found myself on the twenty-fourth twiddling my thumbs and watching Korean TV soaps while others were out partridging in pear trees. I scowled at the screen, unsympathetic toward the pretty Korean brides harassed by their in-laws. I was in a foul, decidedly un-Christmassy mood.

By the afternoon of the twenty-fifth I had started to unravel and unpack, throwing things all over the carpet. I would stay locked in my flat, I decided, reading trashy novels and doing nothing. I began to look forward to this silly but restful indolence, a form of holiday I had not enjoyed for at least a year.

Ko Sonny called that evening.

"We have tickets for tomorrow. Do you still want to come? Are you

Defiled on the Ayeyarwaddy

ready?"

Do I ever. Am I ever.

While I was waiting for Ko Sonny to pick me up the next morning, the phone rang. It was my "adopted" son Kyaw Thura wishing me a Merry Christmas and checking to see if I was hung over. We had met many years ago under strange circumstances— i.e., politics and Insein Prison—and each had liked the way the other handled it, with equal aplomb. With mischief, even. After that event blew over, we had sort of "adopted" each other as we seemed cut from the same cloth.

Kyaw is the protective sort and feels strongly that his "mom" should not be allowed to gallivant alone all over the country, or in the company of men who are not relatives, so unless caught in the act I never tell him beforehand when I plan a trip. It would not do to tell him that I was just about to go to Myitkyina to drink and dance at a Kachin festival. He knows I love rice wine fermenting in pots, ever since he once caught sight of me at a party clutching one of those pots, not letting anyone else near it.

We chatted about Christmas parties he had been to the previous day, and he sounded pleased that for once I stayed home. I did not tell him why. Then I heard the horn of Ko Sonny's car.

"Oops, someone at the door," I said, "Gotta go, sweetie. I'll call you later. Take care."

The Ayeyarwaddy River starts a few miles north of Myitkyina, at the confluence of the Mai Kha and Mali Kha rivers. I had always wanted to float down the Ayeyarwaddy on canoes, rafts, barges, or steamers, but so far had only managed a trip from Bhamo to Mandalay to Bagan on a series of passenger boats. After attending the Manau, I had vague hopes of traveling all the way down the river...

THINGSASIAN PRESS

Experience Asia Through the Eyes of Travelers

"To know the road ahead, ask those coming back."
(CHINESE PROVERB)

East meets West at ThingsAsian Press, where the secrets of
Asia are revealed by the travelers who know them best. Writers
who have lived and worked in Asia. Writers with stories to tell
about basking on the beaches of Thailand, teaching English
conversation in the exclusive salons of Tokyo, trekking in
Bhutan, haggling with antique vendors in the back alleys of
Shanghai, eating spicy noodles on the streets of Jakarta,
photographing the children of Nepal, cycling the length of
Vietnam's Highway One, traveling through Laos on the mighty
Mekong, and falling in love on the island of Kyushu.

Inspired by the many expert, adventurous and independent
contributors who helped us build **ThingsAsian.com**, our
publications are intended for both active travelers and those
who journey vicariously, on the wings of words.

ThingsAsian Press specializes in travel stories, photo journals,
cultural anthologies, destination guides and children's books.
We are dedicated to assisting readers in exploring the cultures
of Asia through the eyes of experienced travelers.

www.thingsasianpress.com